GROW TOGETHER NOW

VOLUME 1

- ❁ FORGIVENESS
- ❁ PEACEMAKING
- ❁ SERVANT'S HEART

Group resources really work!

This Group resource incorporates our R.E.A.L. approach to ministry. It reinforces a growing friendship with Jesus, encourages long-term learning, and results in life transformation, because it's

Relational
Learner-to-learner interaction enhances learning and builds Christian friendships.

Experiential
What learners experience through discussion and action sticks with them up to 9 times longer than what they simply hear or read.

Applicable
The aim of Christian education is to equip learners to be both hearers and doers of God's Word.

Learner-based
Learners understand and retain more when the learning process takes into consideration how they learn best.

Grow Together Now, Volume 1
Copyright © 2017 Group Publishing, Inc./0000 0001 0362 4853

Visit our website: **group.com**

All rights reserved. No part of this book may be reproduced in any manner whatsoever without prior written permission from the publisher, except where noted in the text and in the case of brief quotations embodied in critical articles and reviews. For information, visit group.com/permissions.

CREDITS
Executive Editor: Jody Brolsma
Assistant Editor: Ann Diaz
Art Director: Veronica Preston
Designer: Andy Towler
Media Production Supervisor/Producer: Michael Freeman
Illustrators: Paige Billin-Frye, David Cabot, Wes Comer, Patrick Creyts,
    iStockphoto.com/jane, iStockPhoto.com/memoangeles, iStockPhoto.com/
    Pushkarevskyy, Pamela Johnson, Dana Regan, Ronnie Rooney

Unless otherwise indicated, all Scripture quotations are taken from the Holy Bible, New Living Translation, copyright © 1996, 2004, 2007, 2013, 2015 by Tyndale House Foundation. Used by permission of Tyndale House Publishers, Inc., Carol Stream, Illinois 60188. All rights reserved.

ISBN 978-1-4707-5110-4

Printed in the United States of America.

10 9 8 7 6 5 4 3 2 1   20 19 18 17

HOW TO USE GROW TOGETHER NOW

Grow Together Now is rooted in Scripture and engages kids to grow to be like Jesus. Use these lessons to equip kids with the character qualities they need to each become the person God created them to be. These exciting, hands-on Bible lessons feature the three character qualities of forgiveness, peacemaking, and having a servant's heart. Kids will explore each character quality in memorable activities that reinforce God's foundational plan for a fruitful Christian life.

With these lessons, you'll introduce kids of all ages to:

- **Forgiveness**—Trusting God to help me love others who hurt me.
- **Peacemaking**—Getting along with others.
- **Servant's heart**—Thinking of others before I think of myself.

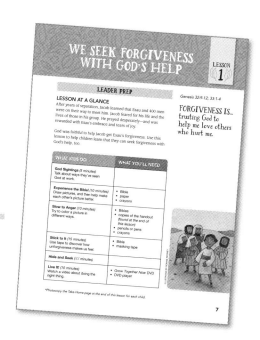

OVERVIEW CHART

This helpful chart gives you an overview of the lesson. Read "What Kids Do" first so you have the big picture of what will happen in your classroom with kids. Use the "What You'll Need" list to review and gather all the supplies you'll need for a great lesson.

DEVOTION FOR TEACHERS

Grow Together Now isn't just for children; it's for you, too! Romans 8:29 says that God chose you "to become like his Son." With this devotion, let God speak to your heart and challenge you to grow in your friendship with him.

BIBLE FOUNDATION FOR TEACHERS

Each lesson includes an in-depth look into the related Bible passage. Allow God's Spirit to work in your heart and mind as you study the Scripture in preparation for your lesson.

THE LESSON

Research shows that people remember most of what they do but only a fraction of what they hear—which means that kids learn best by doing. Kids will act out skits, make things, create prayers, play games, do experiments, and actively participate in conversations to discover important biblical truths. Each lesson has the following features, plus more.

GOD SIGHTINGS

Talk about ways you've each seen God at work, and praise him!

BIBLE EXPLORATION

Dive into the Scripture with kids, and learn by doing a unique activity to drive home the point.

LIFE APPLICATION

Reinforce the message with an experience designed to help kids apply God's Word to their lives.

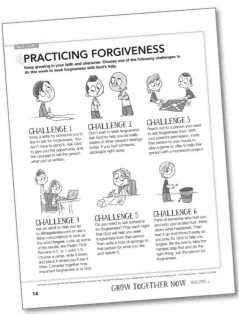

TAKE-HOME PAGE

Each week, kids will get six challenges on the Take-Home page. Encourage kids to choose at least one challenge to grow in character throughout the week. Let parents know that they can ask their children about the challenge and help when necessary.

TABLE OF CONTENTS

LESSON 1 — We Seek Forgiveness With God's Help 7
Genesis 32:9-12; 33:1-4: Esau Forgives Jacob

LESSON 2 — God Wants Us to Show Forgiveness to Others 17
Matthew 18:21-35: Jesus Tells About the Unmerciful Servant

LESSON 3 — We Can Forgive Others as We've Been Forgiven 27
Mark 2:1-12: Jesus Heals a Paralyzed Man

LESSON 4 — Anyone Can Be Forgiven 37
Acts 9:1-19: Saul's Conversion on the Road to Damascus

LESSON 5 — God Helps Us Get Along With Our Families 47
Genesis 13:1-18: Abram and Lot Work Out Their Differences

LESSON 6 — We Make Peace 57
Genesis 31:4-55: Laban Pursues Jacob

LESSON 7 — We Pray When People Are Mean 65
Nehemiah 4:1-9: Enemies Threaten Nehemiah

LESSON 8 — God Gives Us Peace 75
Matthew 6:25-34: Jesus Teaches About Peace

LESSON 9 — We Bring Peace 83
Philemon 1:4-22: Onesimus Returns to Philemon

LESSON 10 — Jesus Wants Us to Serve Others 91
Matthew 20:20-28: The Disciples Argue

LESSON 11 — We Can Serve Others as Jesus Did 101
John 13:1-17: Jesus Washes the Disciples' Feet

LESSON 12 — We Serve God With Our Family 109
Joshua 24:14-18: Joshua's Family Serves God

LESSON 13 — We Serve Everyone 119
Luke 10:30-37: The Good Samaritan

WE SEEK FORGIVENESS WITH GOD'S HELP

LESSON 1

LEADER PREP

Genesis 32:9-12; 33:1-4

LESSON AT A GLANCE

After years of separation, Jacob learned that Esau and 400 men were on their way to meet him. Jacob feared for his life and the lives of those in his group. He prayed desperately—and was rewarded with Esau's embrace and tears of joy.

God was faithful to help Jacob get Esau's forgiveness. Use this lesson to help children learn that they can seek forgiveness with God's help, too.

FORGIVENESS IS... trusting God to help me love others who hurt me.

WHAT KIDS DO	WHAT YOU'LL NEED
God Sightings *(5 minutes)* Talk about ways they've seen God at work.	
Explore the Bible! *(10 minutes)* Draw pictures, and then help make each other's picture better.	• Bible • paper • crayons
Slow to Anger *(10 minutes)* Try to color a picture in different ways.	• Bibles • copies of the handout *(found at the end of this lesson)* • pencils or pens • crayons
Stick to It *(15 minutes)* Use tape to discover how unforgiveness makes us feel.	• Bible • masking tape
Hide and Seek *(10 minutes)* Play a game to understand how we have to seek forgiveness.	
Live It! *(10 minutes)* Watch a video about doing the right thing.	• *Grow Together Now* DVD • DVD player

*Photocopy the Take-Home page at the end of this lesson for each child.

ILLUSTRATED BY RONNIE ROONEY

DEVOTIONS FOR LEADERS: FORGIVENESS

No one looks forward to facing those they've hurt. However, we can learn how to do it from Jacob. First, pray. In your prayers, remember God and his promises. Humble yourself, making your requests known to God. Be honest about your fears, and choose to trust him. Then go. Face what you've done and the person you've wronged. Just as Jacob never expected the kind of reception he got from his brother, so too your fears might be all for nothing. Jacob not only got Esau's forgiveness but he also got his brother back.

BIBLE BACKGROUND FOR LEADERS

Genesis 32:9-12; 33:1-4: Esau Forgives Jacob

CAUGHT RED-HANDED

Jacob was terrified at the prospect of reuniting with his older brother, Esau. After all, the last time they were in the same place, Esau was plotting to kill him (Genesis 27:42). It all started when Jacob stole his brother's blessing. On the surface that might not seem like a big deal—but in Jewish culture, there was nothing more important than this blessing, especially if you were the firstborn son. In *The Blessing*, Gary Smalley and John Trent point out that firstborns received the privilege of marrying first and receiving a double portion of inheritance. Once the father passed away, the firstborn son assumed leadership of the family. In a wealthy family like Isaac's, Esau's life seemed secure. Therefore, Jacob didn't steal a tender gesture from his brother—in essence, he stole Esau's future.

WHEN IN DOUBT, PRAY

As Jacob journeyed homeward, he saw his brother coming toward him with 400 men. However, rather than fleeing, Jacob chose to pray. First, he remembered who God is: "[the] God of my grandfather Abraham, and God of my father, Isaac." Second, Jacob reminded God of his commands and promises: "You told me, 'Return to your own land...' And You promised me, 'I will treat you kindly.'" Third, he humbled himself: "I am not worthy of all the unfailing love and faithfulness you have shown to me." Next, he asked for God's help: "O Lord, please rescue me from the hand of my brother, Esau." Then he spoke to God honestly: "I am afraid that he is coming to attack me, along with my wives and

children." Finally, he ended by trusting God's commitment: "You promised me, 'I will surely treat you kindly, and I will multiply your descendants.' "

HOMECOMING

After Jacob's all-nighter in the wrestling ring, he still feared Esau's arrival. Jacob sent messengers with explicit instructions on what to say; he sent gifts of animals; he even arranged his family in a specific order. It was as if he wanted to physically show Esau how sorry he was, even before speaking a word. At last, Jacob faced Esau. Humbly, Jacob bowed to the ground seven times. Esau, for his part, ran to him, embraced him, and kissed him—a reception reminiscent of a story that Jesus told about another younger son, a prodigal, who had wrongfully taken an inheritance but who finally returned home.

THE LESSON

GOD SIGHTINGS

Say: **God is with us everywhere! When your friend shares with you, you feel God's kindness. When you smile at a stranger and hold open a door, you're being God at work. A beautiful sunset is evidence of God's creativity and power. It's important that we recognize and thank God for all the things he does in our lives. We call these God Sightings.**

Ask: **What evidence have you seen of God at work this week? Think about God's creation, ways people have encouraged you, and even ways God helped you make a difference for someone else.**

Share your own God Sighting first. Then let kids share God Sightings—evidence of God in our world. Then celebrate how God is at work in your lives through a prayer of thanksgiving.

LESSON 1 | WE SEEK FORGIVENESS WITH GOD'S HELP

YOU'LL NEED:

✓ **Bible**
✓ **paper**
✓ **crayons**

EXPLORE THE BIBLE!

Talk about: **The Bible tells us about two brothers, Jacob and Esau. In what we're reading today from the Bible, the brothers hadn't seen each other in a long time. Before this time, Jacob had done something mean to trick Esau. He'd done something wrong and hadn't asked for forgiveness.**

Give each child crayons and paper. Have kids fold their paper in half and then in half again, creating four sections.

Talk about: **After I read some verses from the Bible, you'll draw in each square what Jacob or Esau did.**

Allow two minutes after each reading for kids to draw.

- Read Genesis 32:9-10.
- Read Genesis 32:11-12.
- Read Genesis 33:1-3.
- Read Genesis 33:4.

Have kids trade pictures. Say: **Ask your partner to help make your picture better by adding in something new.** *(Pause.)* **Help each other, and see what you come up with.**

Afterward, lead this discussion: **How did your partner help make your picture better? What did God do in this Scripture that seemed most helpful? In what ways can God help you when you feel worried or sad?**

Talk about: **Your partner helped, but you had to do something first. You had to ask for help. Jacob thought Esau was coming to hurt him, so he prayed to God and asked for help. Jacob bowed, showing how sorry he was, and Esau forgave his brother immediately.** *We seek forgiveness with God's help.* **Let's explore more about what forgiveness is and why it's so important.**

SLOW TO ANGER

Distribute handouts and pens or pencils. Say: **God helped Jacob ask his brother, Esau, for forgiveness.**

At the top of your handout, write or draw about a time someone surprised you by forgiving you unexpectedly.

Read Psalm 145:8. Explain that "compassionate" means kind or sympathetic. Set out crayons and say: **In the first box on your handout, quickly and angrily color the picture with back and forth strokes across the page.** Allow 10 seconds.

Then say: **Now color again. In the second box, move your hand slowly and gently to color in the picture.** Allow time.

Then talk about: **How would you describe the coloring job you did the first time? How does this experience remind you of what happens when we react with anger?**

Say: **God is slow to get angry and filled with unfailing love. When we do bad things, we can ask for forgiveness.**

Lead this discussion: **How does God's forgiveness show that he's compassionate or kind? Why is it sometimes hard to seek forgiveness from someone you've hurt? How can God help when we need to ask for forgiveness?**

Say: **Think about someone you've hurt and how you can ask that person for forgiveness. Remember that God will help you!** *We seek forgiveness with God's help.*

YOU'LL NEED:

- ✓ **Bible**
- ✓ **copies of the handout** *(found at the end of this lesson)*
- ✓ **pens or pencils**
- ✓ **crayons**

STICK TO IT

Say: **Jacob knew he hurt Esau and wanted forgiveness from him with God's help. With a partner, talk about the last time you asked someone for forgiveness.**

While kids talk, distribute strips of masking tape. Then give these directions: **Wrap masking tape around your wrist with the sticky side facing out. Walk around the room, naming at least five things that people have done to you that you've had to forgive, such as break something you own. Each**

YOU'LL NEED:

- ✓ **Bible**
- ✓ **masking tape**

LESSON 1 | WE SEEK FORGIVENESS WITH GOD'S HELP

time you name something, touch something in the room with your sticky tape.

After several minutes, lead this discussion: **Take a look at how much dirt or fuzz you collected on your tape. How is the stuff on your tape like or unlike what happens to a relationship that needs forgiveness?**

Say: **Your tape gathered a lot of junk, much like relationships pick up extra junk along the way when we're not careful. In any argument, there are always two sides. God helps us admit our own mistakes, and when we admit we're wrong, others can forgive us.** *We seek forgiveness with God's help.*

Find a partner and talk about this: What's one thing you can do this week to fix a problem you're having with someone?

Share your own example first. Then let kids share with a partner. Then say: **Let's play a game to explore something more about forgiveness.**

HIDE AND SEEK

Choose one person to be the Seeker. Have everyone else hide in the classroom while the Seeker covers his or her eyes and counts to 20. (You may need to move outside or to a larger room for this activity.)

Wait until the Seeker finds everyone. Then switch roles so everyone can be the Seeker.

Then talk about: **How is searching for other people like seeking forgiveness?**

Say: **Forgiveness doesn't just fall into our laps. We seek it out and ask for it. When we've wronged someone, we seek forgiveness with God's help.**

LIVE IT!

Say: **Okay, race fans. It's time to strap on your helmets, get a little dirty, and pick your favorite team color. Here's the American Grand Prix!**

Show "Choose Your Own Adventure" (track 1) from the *Grow Together Now* DVD. Pause the video when told to.

Lead this discussion: **What did you think of the race? Talk about a time you've seen someone cheating. What do you do when someone cheats?**

After discussion, show the rest of the video.

Then talk about: **Justin knew he made a bad choice. He knew he couldn't accept the win because he had cheated. Instead of lying to cover it up, he said he was sorry and asked forgiveness. In the same way, when we make bad choices, *we seek forgiveness with God's help*.**

PRAYER
Dear God, thank you for helping us when we need to ask forgiveness. No matter how hard it is, we know we can do it with your help. In Jesus' name, amen.

TAKE-HOME PAGE

Give each child a Take-Home page. Encourage kids to select one of the six challenges for the week ahead.

TAKE-HOME

PRACTICING FORGIVENESS

Keep growing in your faith and character. Choose one of the following challenges to do this week to seek forgiveness with God's help.

CHALLENGE 1
Write a letter to someone you'd like to ask for forgiveness. You don't have to send it. Ask God to give you the opportunity and the courage to tell the person what you've written.

CHALLENGE 2
Don't wait to seek forgiveness. Ask God to help you be really aware of other people's feelings today. If you hurt someone, apologize right away.

CHALLENGE 3
Reach out to a person you need to ask forgiveness from. With your parent's permission, invite that person to your house to play a game or offer to help that person with a homework project.

CHALLENGE 4
Ask an adult to help you go to Biblegateway.com or use a Bible concordance to look up the word *forgive*. Look up some of the results, like Psalm 79:9; Romans 4:7; or 1 John 1:9. Choose a verse, write it down, and place it where you'll see it often. Consider together how important forgiveness is to God.

CHALLENGE 5
Do you need to ask someone for forgiveness? Pray each night that God will help you seek forgiveness from that person. Then write a note of apology to that person for what you did, and deliver it.

CHALLENGE 6
Think of someone who hurt you and who you've also hurt. Write down what happened. Then tear it up and throw it away as you pray for God to help you forgive. Be the one to take the hardest step first and do the right thing: Ask the person for forgiveness.

Permission to photocopy this resource from Grow Together Now, Volume 1 granted for local church use. Copyright © Group Publishing, Inc., 1515 Cascade Ave., Loveland, CO 80538.

GROW TOGETHER NOW VOLUME 1

SLOW TO ANGER

Directions: Write or draw about a time someone surprised you by forgiving you unexpectedly.

LESSON 1 | WE SEEK FORGIVENESS WITH GOD'S HELP

GOD WANTS US TO SHOW FORGIVENESS TO OTHERS

LESSON 2

LEADER PREP

Matthew 18:21-35

LESSON AT A GLANCE

Jesus challenged his disciples to offer extravagant forgiveness. Then he used a parable to help them understand they'd been forgiven greatly by God. He even emphasized the point by communicating the consequences for those who've received God's forgiveness and yet refuse to forgive others. Use this lesson to help children learn to show forgiveness to others.

FORGIVENESS IS...
trusting God to help me love others who hurt me.

WHAT KIDS DO	WHAT YOU'LL NEED
God Sightings *(5 minutes)* Talk about ways they've seen God at work.	
Explore the Bible! *(10 minutes)* Watch a video about forgiveness.	• Bibles • *Grow Together Now* DVD • DVD player • paper • pencils
Wall Press *(15 minutes)* Experience relief after pressing against a wall; then draw or write about how forgiveness feels.	• Bible • copies of the handout *(found at the end of this lesson)* • crayons or pencils • timer
Carrying Debt *(10 minutes)* See how carrying "debt" slows them down.	• Bible • tennis ball • timer
Sing It Out *(10 minutes)* Write a forgiveness song.	• newsprint • marker • musical instrument *(optional)*
Live It! *(10 minutes)* Think about how mistakes harm us and other people.	• modeling clay • pencils

ILLUSTRATED BY DREW ROSE

*Photocopy the Take-Home page at the end of this lesson for each child.

DEVOTIONS FOR LEADERS: FORGIVENESS

Think right now of any grudges you may be holding—big ones like anger and bitterness you're holding on to, or small ones like a persistent sense of annoyance with a child. Choose one and write it down somewhere. Then use your imagination to place yourself inside Jesus' parable. The grudge you wrote down is the "debt" someone owes you…but how big is the debt you owe the King? Spend time today reflecting on the depth and immensity of God's forgiveness toward you. Let that forgiveness and grace motivate you to truly forgive the person you wrote about. (If you've been hurt deeply in your past, seek the help of a counselor or pastor to begin the forgiveness process.)

BIBLE BACKGROUND FOR LEADERS

Matthew 18:21-35: Jesus Tells About the Unmerciful Servant

JESUS TELLS A PARABLE

Jesus had just finished outlining for the disciples the game plan to use when a Christian sins against them, describing several steps Christians should take to try to reconcile (verses 15-20). Jesus challenged his followers to go above and beyond in their efforts to reconcile with other Christians when conflict arises. As a follow-up, Peter asked for some clarification, wondering how far our forgiveness should go (verse 21). Jesus answered with a parable describing the values of God's kingdom. In this story, the king (representing God) forgave a servant's tremendous financial debt. But instead of responding with grace, this forgiven servant refused to forgive another man who owed him a much smaller amount. When the king learned of the first servant's lack of forgiveness, he sentenced him to what amounts to a lifetime of imprisonment.

PETER ASKS A QUESTION

When Peter asked Jesus how often he should forgive, he wasn't trying to cut corners or do the bare minimum. In fact, Pharisaical teachings of the time taught that an especially righteous person would forgive three times—but Peter suggested seven times. This symbolically represented completeness and was more than double the Pharisee's norm. Peter's idea of how forgiving a Christian should be was already pretty amazing. But Jesus calls

ILLUSTRATED BY DANA REGAN

his followers to an exponentially higher degree of forgiveness: "Seventy times seven!" (Matthew 18:22). And his parable takes it one step further, clearly communicating a poignant truth: We, like the first servant, have received amazing, extravagant forgiveness from God. How can we withhold forgiveness from another person?

BRINGING IT TOGETHER

We're faced with the decision to forgive or not forgive countless times every week, from how we'll regard the rude stranger who cut in front of us in line to how we'll respond to a family member who has purposefully said something hurtful. In cases like these, withholding forgiveness can usually seem pretty justified. It's easy to come up with decent, logical reasons for harboring a grudge or standing in judgment over someone else. In this Scripture, though, Peter sets the bar high, and Jesus sets it many notches higher. He calls his followers to a degree of forgiveness that defies human logic. He calls us, his followers, to live—and forgive—in a way that stands out from the crowd.

THE LESSON

GOD SIGHTINGS

Use the standard text provided or substitute your own examples for this weekly lesson-starter activity.

Say: **God is with us everywhere! When your friend shares with you, you feel God's kindness. When you smile at a stranger and hold open a door, you're being God at work. A beautiful sunset is evidence of God's creativity and power. It's important that we recognize and thank God for all the things he does in our lives. We call these God Sightings.**

Ask: **What evidence have you seen of God at work this week? Think about God's creation, ways people have encouraged you, and even ways God helped you make a difference for someone else.**

Share your own God Sighting first. Then let kids share God Sightings—evidence of God in our world. Then celebrate how God is at work in your lives through a prayer of thanksgiving.

LESSON 2 | GOD WANTS US TO SHOW FORGIVENESS TO OTHERS

YOU'LL NEED:

✓ **Bibles**
✓ *Grow Together Now* **DVD**
✓ **DVD player**
✓ **paper**
✓ **pencils**

YOU'LL NEED:

✓ **Bible**
✓ **copies of the handout** (found at the end of this lesson)
✓ **crayons or pencils**
✓ **timer**

EXPLORE THE BIBLE!

Say: **In the Bible, Jesus sometimes used stories to help people understand something. Today we'll look at a story Jesus told when someone asked about how many times we *really* have to forgive others.**

Read aloud Matthew 18:21-35.

Then say: **Now that you've *heard* Jesus' story, let's *see* it in a fresh, fun way!** Show "The Paper Parable" (track 2) from the *Grow Together Now* DVD.

Talk about: **Now it's your turn to come up with a story about forgiveness, maybe something that could happen today. Try to include the elements of crime and punishment that Jesus had in his story. If you want to refer to Jesus' story, you can find it in Matthew 18:21-35.**

Distribute Bibles, paper, and pencils, and allow time for kids to write their stories. Allow them to work individually or together. Then have willing kids read their stories out loud. If they aren't comfortable reading out loud, have them give you their stories to read silently.

Lead this discussion: **What did Jesus' story and the ones we just wrote show us about forgiveness? When have you had an opportunity to forgive someone and not done so?** Share an example from your own life first, and then let kids share their stories. **Why is forgiveness so important?**

Talk about: **In Jesus' story, the king represents God, and the first man represents us. God has forgiven us for so much! In the same way,** *God wants us to show forgiveness to others.*

WALL PRESS

Say: **Jesus' parable about the unforgiving servant tells us that God has forgiven us, and he wants us to forgive others. It also helps us think about the consequences of not forgiving others.** Ask for volunteers to explain the word *consequences*.

Next, have kids find a place to stand against a wall with their arms at their sides. Go into the hallway if necessary for plenty of space.

Say: **Now turn so that your right side is toward the wall. When I say "go," I want you to press your arm against the wall as hard as you possibly can. Don't stop pressing until the timer runs out.** Start the timer for one minute.

When one minute is up, have kids take a few steps away from the wall and relax.

Lead this discussion: **Say one word that tells how it felt to step away from the wall. How is forgiveness like stepping away from the wall?**

Talk about: **God wants us to show forgiveness to others when we feel angry or hurt, and then we can be light and free. When we hold on to unforgiveness, it hurts us more than it hurts the person we're not forgiving. When we forgive others, we feel a lot better.**

Distribute handouts and crayons or pencils. Say: **On your handout, make two lists of emotions: those you experience when someone treats you badly, and those you experience when you forgive someone. You can make a list of words or draw emojis. For example, you could draw a smiley face to represent being happy or a dark cloud to represent being angry.** Allow time. Then let kids share their work with a partner.

Say: **Being mad at someone, even if the person has treated us badly, makes us feel bad. But it's such a good feeling to forgive and get rid of that pain. Jesus had some surprising things to say about how to treat people who hurt us.**

Read Luke 6:27-31. Lead this discussion: **How do the actions in these verses demonstrate forgiveness? Which of these verses do you think would be the most difficult to live out, and why? What's one thing you can do today to demonstrate forgiveness?**

Say: **The servant was wrong because he refused to forgive the other servant, even though he'd been forgiven a much larger debt. God forgives us just as the king forgave the servant. And because he forgives us, we forgive others, too.** *God wants us to show forgiveness to others.*

> **LEADER TIP**
>
> Younger children have a keenly developed sense of what is and isn't fair. Given that forgiveness, in many ways, isn't fair, they may have difficulty understanding that forgiveness is something much deeper than fairness. It's something without limits. Look for opportunities to help children who are struggling with feeling treated unfairly; help shape children's character by reminding them that forgiveness isn't about being treated the same as others, but it's about letting go of the hurt when we're treated differently.

LESSON 2 | GOD WANTS US TO SHOW FORGIVENESS TO OTHERS

YOU'LL NEED:

- ✓ Bible
- ✓ tennis ball
- ✓ timer

CARRYING DEBT

Say: **In the parable of the unforgiving servant, Jesus uses debts—owing someone money—to represent sins that need to be forgiven. Jesus even included forgiveness as part of prayer. Listen.**

Read aloud Matthew 6:12. Talk about: **In what ways are debts like or unlike sins?**

Then give kids time to reflect quietly on the following questions: **What "debts" has God forgiven for you?** (Allow time.) **What "debts" do you have to forgive for others?**

Have kids get into one line on one side of the room. Explain that they will speed walk from one side of the room to the other and that you'll time the group from start to finish (not individually). Time them the first time as they speed walk freely. Invite any child with a physical limitation to be a timer.

The second time, tell kids they'll have to balance a tennis ball on two fingers, knuckles up, as they go. Say: **If the ball gets away from you, pick it up, go back to where you left off, and then continue.** Time the group again.

Talk about: **Why did you go faster the first time?**

Say: **Not forgiving someone means refusing to let go of your anger and your desire to punish someone. And it's like balancing a ball—you can't always control it, and it slows you down. You can't really enjoy life when you choose not to forgive.**

Have kids get into pairs or trios to discuss:

- Think about a time you forgave someone even though it was difficult. How did you feel before and after you forgave that person?

- How can we know when we have forgiven someone from the heart?

Ask for volunteers to share with the larger group their responses to the last question. Then say: **Forgiveness can be hard, especially when we feel really hurt by what someone did** to us. But God forgives us when we hurt him. *God wants us to show forgiveness to others.*

SING IT OUT

Gather everyone around a large sheet of newsprint taped to the wall or a dry-erase board.

Say: **Let's write a short, rhyming poem together about forgiveness.**

Encourage kids to contribute lines to the poem, and write the words where everyone can see them.

Together, sing the poem in a commercial-jingle style. Play an instrument such as a guitar, tambourine, or maracas to keep the beat. Or simply have kids clap or snap to the beat.

Say: **It's not always easy to forgive. This song can help us remember how important it is to God that we forgive, and we can ask him to help us.** *God wants us to show forgiveness to others.*

YOU'LL NEED:

✓ **newsprint**
✓ **marker**
✓ **musical instrument** (optional)

LIVE IT!

Give each child some modeling clay and a pencil. Say: **Make a sculpture of yourself. Try to make it perfect with no bumps or mistakes.** Allow time.

Say: **Think of some things you've done wrong that have hurt God or other people. For each thing you think of, make a mark in your sculpture with your pencil.** Pause while kids make marks. If they stop after a few marks, encourage them to think of more things they've done.

Say: **When we make mistakes, God forgives us. Roll your clay back into a ball and make your sculpture brand new.** Pause while children create.

Say: **Now think of one thing someone else has done to hurt you that's hard to forgive. Make a mark in your sculpture to represent that thing.** Pause while kids make their marks.

YOU'LL NEED:

✓ **modeling clay**
✓ **pencils**

LESSON 2 | GOD WANTS US TO SHOW FORGIVENESS TO OTHERS

Lead this discussion: **How does thinking about God's forgiveness help you forgive? What'll it take for you to forgive the things you made marks about?**

Talk about: **God has forgiven us for so much. It's like the ten thousand talents the king in Jesus' story forgave. But sometimes, we have a hard time forgiving one little thing.**

We saw the punishment the man in Jesus' story faced for not forgiving. Let's follow God's loving example. *God wants us to show forgiveness to others.*

PRAYER
Thank you, God, for your forgiveness. As we remember the forgiveness you have given us, help us be forgiving toward others. In Jesus' name, amen.

TAKE-HOME PAGE

Give each child a Take-Home page. Encourage kids to select one of the six challenges for the week ahead.

PRACTICING FORGIVENESS

Keep growing in your faith and character. Choose one of the following challenges to do this week to show forgiveness to others.

CHALLENGE 1
One of the hardest people for us to forgive is ourselves. It's easy to get mad at ourselves when we do something we know we shouldn't. Think about what it means to forgive yourself for doing wrong. Then take time to pray that God would help you extend forgiveness to yourself.

CHALLENGE 2
Place a jar and several squares of paper somewhere in your room. When someone does something wrong toward you, write a brief description of what happened on a piece a paper. Pray that God will help you forgive that person from the heart. Then tear up the paper and drop the pieces in the jar as a symbol that you have forgiven him or her.

CHALLENGE 3
Genesis 37–50 tells about Joseph being sold into slavery by his brothers and then being taken to Egypt. Read Genesis 50:15-21. Make a list of things you can learn about forgiving others from the way Joseph responded to his brothers. Then choose one of them to put into practice today.

CHALLENGE 4
Watch for times throughout your day when someone does something to hurt or annoy you. Try not to say anything in response. Instead, take a moment to pray for that person, forgiving him or her in your heart and asking God to let that person experience his love today.

CHALLENGE 5
Read The Lord's Prayer (Matthew 6:9-13). When you get to the section about forgiveness, take time to thank God for things he has forgiven you for and to forgive those who have wronged you.

CHALLENGE 6
Ask your parents or another adult to tell you about a time they had to forgive someone and what they learned from that experience.

LESSON 2 | GOD WANTS US TO SHOW FORGIVENESS TO OTHERS

HANDOUT

HOW I FEEL WHEN...

HOW I FEEL WHEN I'M TREATED BADLY

HOW I FEEL WHEN I FORGIVE SOMEONE

Permission to photocopy this resource from Grow Together Now, Volume 1 granted for local church use. Copyright © Group Publishing, Inc., 1515 Cascade Ave., Loveland, CO 80538.

WE CAN FORGIVE OTHERS AS WE'VE BEEN FORGIVEN

LESSON 3

LEADER PREP

Mark 2:1-12

LESSON AT A GLANCE
Some friends brought a paralyzed man to Jesus so he could be healed—but before healing him, Jesus forgave all his sins. God's forgiveness of us is an amazing gift. And God tells us to share that gift with others. Use this lesson to help children learn to forgive others as they've been forgiven.

FORGIVENESS IS...
trusting God to help me love others who hurt me.

WHAT KIDS DO	WHAT YOU'LL NEED
God Sightings *(5 minutes)* Talk about ways they've seen God at work.	
Explore the Bible! *(10 minutes)* Watch a video about forgiveness.	• Bible • *Grow Together Now* DVD • DVD player
Wipe Away Sins *(10 minutes)* Experience how Jesus can wipe away our wrongs.	• mirror • washable markers • spray bottles with water • paper towels • reflective music
That's Amazing! *(10 minutes)* Consider how accomplishments can't get them into heaven.	• Bible • copies of the handout *(found at the end of this lesson)* • pens or pencils
Tangled Up *(10 minutes)* Explore how being tangled is like unforgiveness.	
Live It! *(10 minutes)* Learn how forgiveness can make things clean.	• glass • water • vinegar • green and red food coloring • bleach • spoon

*Photocopy the Take-Home page at the end of this lesson for each child.

27

DEVOTIONS FOR LEADERS: FORGIVENESS

Jesus came to earth and sacrificed himself on the cross so people could be forgiven of their sins. It's easy to harbor anger toward those who have wronged us, but God wants us to remember his great gift and share his forgiveness with others. Today, think about how Jesus forgave the paralytic's sin. Find ways to demonstrate that same forgiveness to others—even those who might not appear to deserve it.

BIBLE BACKGROUND FOR LEADERS

Mark 2:1-12: Jesus Heals a Paralyzed Man

FOUR PERSISTENT FRIENDS

When Jesus returned to Capernaum from a short trip to Galilee, crowds of people flocked to the place where he stayed. Jesus' reputation as a teacher and a healer had become widespread, so the crowd that came to Jesus filled the house completely. There wasn't even room to get in the door! While Jesus preached to the crowd, four men arrived carrying a mat holding their paralyzed friend. They'd heard about Jesus' ability to heal and desired the same kind of healing for their paralytic companion. However, there wasn't enough room to bring him in, so the friends made a hole in the roof and lowered the man down to Jesus.

ILLUSTRATED BY PAMELA JOHNSON

FORGIVENESS AND A MIRACLE

The persistence the four friends demonstrated revealed their faith that Jesus could heal the paralytic. Jesus recognized this faith and told the paralyzed man that his sins were forgiven. The "teachers of religious law" who were present immediately became angry at Jesus' words. They called Jesus a blasphemer for presuming he could forgive sins. To prove that he had authority from God, Jesus turned to the paralyzed man and healed him. Everyone present, including the teachers of the law, was stunned at this miracle.

JESUS' PURPOSE ON EARTH

This story is an excellent illustration of the authority Jesus has to forgive sins. Romans 5:8 tells us that Jesus came to earth for the purpose of dying for the sins of the whole world. The Bible calls us to extend that same grace to others, forgiving them just as Jesus forgives us.

THE LESSON

GOD SIGHTINGS

Use the standard text provided or substitute your own examples for this weekly lesson-starter activity.

Say: **God is with us everywhere! When your friend shares with you, you feel God's kindness. When you smile at a stranger and hold open a door, you're being God at work. A beautiful sunset is evidence of God's creativity and power. It's important that we recognize and thank God for all the things he does in our lives. We call these God Sightings.**

Ask: **What evidence have you seen of God at work this week? Think about God's creation, ways people have encouraged you, and even ways God helped you make a difference for someone else.**

Share your own God Sighting first. Then let kids share God Sightings—evidence of God in our world. Then celebrate how God is at work in your lives through a prayer of thanksgiving.

EXPLORE THE BIBLE!

Say: **Today we'll explore a surprising Bible story about someone who came to Jesus hoping for one thing but got something even better! Check this out!**

Read aloud Mark 2:1-12.

Ask: **Why do you think Jesus told the paralyzed man that his sins were forgiven?**

Talk about: **Have you ever messed up—I mean made a really big mistake, where you hurt someone's feelings pretty badly? You don't have to share it out loud. Just think on that for a few seconds.** Pause. **We all have! When we mess up, we want people to forgive us. And when other people hurt our feelings, God tells us to forgive them, too. Today let's see how Jesus forgave a man in the Bible.**

Show "A Hole-y Find" (track 3) from the *Grow Together Now* DVD.

YOU'LL NEED:

✓ **Bible**
✓ ***Grow Together Now* DVD**
✓ **DVD player**

LESSON 3 | WE CAN FORGIVE OTHERS AS WE'VE BEEN FORGIVEN

Lead this discussion: **What were some ways you saw forgiveness in this video? Tell about a time someone forgave you. Tell about someone you need to forgive.**

Talk about: **In this story, Jesus showed that he has the power to forgive sins. Only God can do that, and Jesus is God's Son. God forgives us, too. God doesn't like it when we disobey him. But God always loves us and forgives us. We can show God's love when we forgive.** *We can forgive others as we've been forgiven.*

WIPE AWAY SINS

Say: **God loves us no matter what we do, but God wants us to ask for forgiveness when we do wrong things. Let's think of some wrong, hurtful, or disobedient things people do that hurt God's heart.**

Set out a mirror that's large enough for everyone to gather around. Then distribute washable markers. Say: **On our mirror, draw or write some of those wrong things—called sins—that you thought of.** Allow time.

Talk about: **What goes through your mind when you look at your reflection in this mirror? How would you feel if you had to see yourself through all these sins every day?**

Then set out spray bottles and paper towels and say: **Now spray the mirror with water. As you wipe away the words and pictures, ask God to forgive you.**

Play about a minute of reflective music while kids clean the mirror.

Say: **When we ask God to forgive us for the wrong things we've done, God forgives us.**

Lead this discussion: **How does the clean mirror remind you of being forgiven? How did Jesus show that forgiveness is the most important thing? How can being forgiven help you forgive others?**

Say: **Just as Jesus forgave the paralyzed man, he's forgiven us. And** *we can forgive others as we've been forgiven.*

YOU'LL NEED:

- ✓ mirror
- ✓ washable markers
- ✓ spray bottles with water
- ✓ paper towels
- ✓ reflective music

GROW TOGETHER NOW VOLUME 1

THAT'S AMAZING!

Distribute handouts and pens or pencils.

Say: **Jesus didn't just forgive the man; he healed the man, too. That's amazing! Think about three of the most amazing accomplishments anyone has ever done in the history of man. Write those three things on your paper.** Allow time, and have kids share with a partner. Then invite them to share with the class.

Say: **Now draw or write about a time someone forgave you.** Allow time.

Talk about: **Gather with two other people and compare the amazing things at the top of your paper to the forgiveness you experienced. Talk about which is more amazing—the things listed or being forgiven—and why.**

Let kids share together for a while; then take a few reports.

Say: **Jesus has the power to do amazing physical things, like heal someone, and amazing spiritual things, like forgive sins! He surprised a lot of people in the Bible.**

Read aloud Mark 2:9-11. Then lead this discussion: **Why did Jesus think it was more important to forgive the man than to heal him? Explain whether you'd rather be forgiven for your sins or healed if you couldn't walk.**

Have kids flip their papers over. Say: **Jesus' most important job—the whole reason he came to earth—was forgiving sins. What do you need Jesus to forgive you for today? Draw or write about that on the back of your paper. You won't be asked to share this with anyone.**

Allow time, and then have kids set their papers aside. Then say: **When Jesus died on the cross, we were given the opportunity to be forgiven for all our sins—we just have to ask for that forgiveness. We can share forgiveness, too. When people do wrong things to us,** *we can forgive others as we've been forgiven.*

YOU'LL NEED:

✓ **Bible**
✓ **copies of the handout** *(found at the end of this lesson)*
✓ **pens or pencils**

LESSON 3 | WE CAN FORGIVE OTHERS AS WE'VE BEEN FORGIVEN

TANGLED UP

Gather everyone in a circle.

Say: **When we sin, our insides can feel like they're tied up in knots. So let's get into a tangle! With both hands, reach out to different people who aren't next to you. Grab hands.**

Once the group is ready, say: **Now try to untangle yourselves by crawling under legs, ducking under arms, and twisting and turning, all without letting go of hands.**

Have the group continue holding hands once everyone is untangled. Lead this discussion: **How is being all tangled up like when we haven't forgiven someone? How is getting untangled like forgiving someone who's hurt you?**

Say: **Being tangled on the outside is like being tangled on the inside. It doesn't feel right. When we don't forgive others, we feel tangled.** *God wants us to show forgiveness to others.*

LIVE IT!

Hold up the glass with the vinegar water so all the children can see it. Ask: **What are some sins people commit that hurt God?** As kids list sins, drip about three or four drops of green food coloring into the vinegar water. Then use the spoon to stir.

Ask: **What are some sins people have committed that have hurt you?** Share an example from your own life to get kids thinking; then have kids share. As they do, drip the red food coloring into the green vinegar water. Stir with the spoon.

Say: **When we sin, it makes our hearts get all yucky, just like the color in this water.** Hold up the glass.

Say: **The same thing happens when others sin against us. But God doesn't want our hearts to look this yucky. God wants to forgive our sins, and he wants us to forgive others.** Pour the bleach into the glass and stir. The green and red colors will disappear. Hold up the glass for all to see.

YOU'LL NEED:

- ✓ glass
- ✓ water
- ✓ vinegar
- ✓ green and red food coloring
- ✓ bleach
- ✓ spoon

Say: **Jesus forgives our sins and makes our hearts clean again. In the same way,** *we can forgive others as we've been forgiven.*

Talk about: **God wants us to have lives and hearts that are pure like the clean water. Since Jesus forgives our sins, we want to share that forgiveness with others.** *We can forgive others as we've been forgiven.*

PRAYER
Thank you, God, for forgiving us and giving us the strength to forgive others. In Jesus' name, amen.

TAKE-HOME PAGE

Give each child a Take-Home page. Encourage kids to select one of the six challenges for the week ahead.

FOR TEACHERS:
Fill the glass about half-full of water. Add vinegar until the glass is almost full, and stir. Set this out of kids' reach. Practice this activity beforehand so you can make sure the food coloring will completely disappear. Depending on the size of your glass, you may need to use only two drops of each color.

LESSON 3 | WE CAN FORGIVE OTHERS AS WE'VE BEEN FORGIVEN

TAKE-HOME

PRACTICING FORGIVENESS

Keep growing in your faith and character. Choose one of the following challenges to do this week to forgive others as you've been forgiven.

CHALLENGE 1
Use a pencil to draw a cross on paper. Show it to a friend, and share that Jesus died on the cross. Erase one of the lines of the cross and say that Jesus' death erased our sin. Then erase the other line and share that we can forgive others as we've been forgiven.

CHALLENGE 2
Make a special gift bag for someone who's hurt your feelings. Each day, pray for the person and put a small gift in the bag, such as a note or piece of candy, each time you pray. Then give the bag to the person and offer your forgiveness.

CHALLENGE 3
Ask an adult to tell you about a time he or she needed to forgive someone and how it felt to forgive that person. Share about someone you want to forgive, and ask the adult for advice. Then do it!

CHALLENGE 4
Learn more about what the Bible says about forgiveness. Search on Biblegateway.com, and choose one Bible verse that talks about forgiveness. Then read it! Try to live out what the verse says all day.

CHALLENGE 5
Write in a journal about someone you want to forgive. Write about why you feel hurt, as well as things you may have done wrong in the situation, too. Ask God to help you forgive that person—and really mean it. Then talk to that person and say that you forgive him or her.

CHALLENGE 6
Write "Forgive!" on a bunch of sticky notes, and put them all around your house. Each time you see one, stop and say a short prayer, asking God who you might forgive and for the strength to do it.

Permission to photocopy this resource from Grow Together Now, Volume 1 granted for local church use. Copyright © Group Publishing, Inc., 1515 Cascade Ave., Loveland, CO 80538.

AMAZING ACCOMPLISHMENTS

Think about three of the most amazing accomplishments anyone has ever done. Write those three things here.

1.

2.

3.

A TIME SOMEONE FORGAVE ME:

LESSON 3 | WE CAN FORGIVE OTHERS AS WE'VE BEEN FORGIVEN

ANYONE CAN BE FORGIVEN

LESSON 4

LEADER PREP

Acts 9:1-19

LESSON AT A GLANCE

Saul wasn't a nice guy. He treated Christians terribly, putting them into prison or even having them stoned to death. But on the road to Damascus, God blinded Saul and spoke to him. Through God's forgiveness and grace, the trajectory of Saul's life completely changed. Use this lesson to help children learn that anyone can be forgiven.

FORGIVENESS IS... trusting God to help me love others who hurt me.

WHAT KIDS DO	WHAT YOU'LL NEED
God Sightings *(5 minutes)* Talk about ways they've seen God at work.	
Explore the Bible! *(10 minutes)* Use balloons to illustrate Saul's conversion.	• Bible • round balloons of 2 different sizes and colors • clear tape • pins
Stone Shoe *(10 minutes)* Experience what receiving forgiveness feels like.	• Bible • small stones
Good Deeds? *(10 minutes)* Consider whether good deeds can free them from sin.	• Bible • pens or pencils • copies of the handout *(found at the end of this lesson)*
Piling On the Sins *(10 minutes)* See how sin weighs us down.	• pile of clothes *(hats, gloves, sweaters, coats, and so on)*
Live It! *(10 minutes)* Watch a video about forgiveness.	• *Grow Together Now* DVD • DVD player

ILLUSTRATED BY PAMELA JOHNSON

*Photocopy the Take-Home page at the end of this lesson for each child.

DEVOTIONS FOR LEADERS: FORGIVENESS

Saul certainly seemed to be an unlikely candidate for salvation. Good thing God thought differently! Jesus was the only way a man like Saul could've received forgiveness. Too often we overlook people who may seem "beyond" the reach of God's mercy and forgiveness. As you prepare for this lesson, ask God to open your eyes to people in your world who need the gift of God's grace. Remember that, no matter who they are, no matter what they've done, they can still be forgiven through Jesus' death and resurrection.

BIBLE BACKGROUND FOR LEADERS

Acts 9:1-19: Saul's Conversion on the Road to Damascus

A BLINDING LIGHT

Prior to his conversion, Saul was a zealous Jew. He did all he could to oppose the name of Jesus, even putting many Christians in prison and casting his vote to put Christians to death (Acts 26:9-11). As Saul traveled to Damascus to arrest Christians, Jesus met him on the road. A light "brighter than the sun" (Acts 26:13) flashed from heaven, and Saul dropped to the ground. When Jesus questioned Saul and told Saul who he was, the truth of all Saul had been denying must've swept through him like a flood. In his zeal for God, Saul had been persecuting those who believed in Jesus, God's own Son! When Saul got up from that confrontation, he found that he was blind and needed assistance the rest of the way to Damascus.

DAYS OF DARKNESS

We can only speculate on what went through Saul's mind as he waited, blind, in Damascus for further instructions. God gave Saul time to think, and after three days, God sent a man named Ananias to heal Saul of his blindness (Acts 9:10-18).

A BIG CHANGE

Why did God choose Saul? God could've used anyone. Perhaps he chose Saul to be a supreme example of how a life can be changed when God enters it. This man went on to write a large portion of the New Testament under his new name—Paul. Although Saul was his Jewish name, Paul was the Roman equivalent by which he became better known.

THE LESSON

GOD SIGHTINGS

Use the standard text provided or substitute your own examples for this weekly lesson-starter activity.

Say: **God is with us everywhere! When your friend shares with you, you feel God's kindness. When you smile at a stranger and hold open a door, you're being God at work. A beautiful sunset is evidence of God's creativity and power. It's important that we recognize and thank God for all the things he does in our lives. We call these God Sightings.**

Ask: **What evidence have you seen of God at work this week? Think about God's creation, ways people have encouraged you, and even ways God helped you make a difference for someone else.**

Share your own God Sighting first. Then let kids share God Sightings—evidence of God in our world. Then celebrate how God is at work in your lives through a prayer of thanksgiving.

LESSON 4 | ANYONE CAN BE FORGIVEN

YOU'LL NEED:

- ✓ Bible
- ✓ round balloons of 2 different sizes and colors *(see Leader Prep box)*
- ✓ clear tape
- ✓ pins

WARNING

Children under 8 years of age can choke on uninflated balloons. Adult supervision required. Discard broken balloons at once. Balloons contain latex, so be aware of any latex allergies in your class.

LEADER PREP

Use a pencil to push a darker colored balloon inside a lighter colored balloon. Leave about 1 inch of the end of the inner balloon protruding from the outside balloon, and inflate the inside balloon. When the inside balloon has been inflated, tie it off and use the pencil to poke the end into the outer balloon. Inflate the outer balloon so that the sides of the balloons aren't touching, and tie it off. Make an "X" on each outer balloon with clear tape. You'll need one set of these balloons for each child.

EXPLORE THE BIBLE!

Say: **The Bible tells us about a man named Saul who didn't like Christians at all.** Explain that the balloons represent Saul. **Saul found ways to hurt people who believed in Jesus. He even put some Christians in jail!** Read aloud Acts 9:1-2.

One day, Saul was on his way to the town of Damascus. Suddenly, a bright light from heaven shone on him and a voice spoke to him. Hand a pin to each child and explain that it represents God. **The voice was God's and told Saul that when Saul hurt Christians, he hurt God, too.**

Read aloud Acts 9:3-19. Say: **Saul was so happy! He believed in Jesus right then, and God forgave all his sins.** Have children stick a pin through the tape on the outer balloon. Only the inner balloon will pop. Say: **Saul was a completely changed person! The old Saul was gone, and a new Saul took over!**

Lead this discussion: **What did you think when the inside balloon popped and changed the way the outside balloon looked? How was the way the balloon changed like how Saul changed when God forgave him? How does God's forgiveness change us from the inside out?**

Say: **When Saul was forgiven, he was changed, too. God sent Jesus to die for our sins, and we can accept His forgiveness just as Saul did.** Saul learned that *anyone can be forgiven.*

GROW TOGETHER NOW VOLUME 1

STONE SHOE

Have kids form pairs or trios. Then read Acts 9:17-18 aloud.

Say: **When Saul met Jesus on the road to Damascus, Jesus changed him. Tell a partner about some ways Jesus has changed you.** Give an example from your own life; then allow time for pairs to share.

Distribute small stones, several per person, and instruct kids to put the stones in their shoes and put their shoes back on. Do the activity with kids; put stones in your shoes as well.

Say: **Now follow these directions.**

- **Stand on one foot.**
- **Walk in a little circle.**
- **Stand on your tiptoes.**
- **Take three steps forward.**
- **Slide to the left.**
- **Crouch and touch the floor.**
- **Take four steps backward.**

Now take off your shoes, remove the stones, and let's do this again. Repeat the directions.

Lead this discussion: **What was it like following the directions the first time with the stones? How about the second time? How was taking the stones out of your shoes like receiving forgiveness?**

Talk about: **The activity wasn't very much fun the first time—the stones made it too uncomfortable! And having sin in our life is just like that. Jesus knew that sin was uncomfortable and we needed his forgiveness. That's why he came to earth to die for us! Because of Jesus,** *anyone can be forgiven.*

YOU'LL NEED:

✓ **Bible**
✓ **small stones**

LESSON 4 | ANYONE CAN BE FORGIVEN

YOU'LL NEED:

✓ **Bible**
✓ **copies of the handout** *(found at the end of this lesson)*
✓ **pens or pencils**

GOOD DEEDS?

Distribute handouts and pens or pencils.

Say: **We all need forgiveness because we all mess up. No one is perfect. That's why God sent Jesus to die for us. In the box on your handout, draw or write a sin someone might commit.** Allow time for kids to write or draw.

Then read aloud John 3:16. Talk about: **What does this verse mean to you?**

Say: **Everyone has sin and needs to be forgiven. But some people go about trying to get forgiveness the wrong way. Think of some good deeds that people might do to get forgiveness. Now write them over the words or picture you drew, so they cover it.**

Allow time. Then lead this discussion: **When you look at your box, do you think the good deeds really cover up or erase the sin? Explain. If these good deeds could wipe away our sin, why did Jesus have to die? Why do you think people can't erase their sins by doing good?**

Direct kids to the bottom of their handouts. Say: **Write or draw how you would explain God's love and forgiveness to someone.** Allow time for kids to write or draw; then have kids form trios and share what they wrote.

Say: **Because of Jesus' death and God's love, *anyone can be forgiven.***

PILING ON THE SINS

YOU'LL NEED:

✓ **pile of clothes** *(gloves, hats, sweaters, coats, scarves, and so on)*

Gather everyone in a circle. Choose one person to be the model.

Ask kids to name sins. For each one named, have the model put on one thing—for example, a glove, sweater, coat, or hat. Continue to have the model put on items until you run out of clothing or sins.

Challenge the model to do jumping jacks with all the clothes on. Have everyone say **"Anyone can be forgiven"** together. Each time your group says it, have the model take off one item of the additional clothing. Ask the model to do a few more jumping jacks to show how much easier it is to move without the extra clothes.

Talk about: **How was the pile of heavy clothing like sin? How does it feel to take off the weight of sin?**

Say: **Sin can weigh us down, but Jesus forgives us when we ask him.** *Anyone can be forgiven.*

LIVE IT!

Talk about: **What would you do if someone did something really nasty to you? Would you be able to forgive that person? Let's watch a story about a girl who thought her brother did something unforgivable.**

Show "Spider Guts" (track 4) from the *Grow Together Now* DVD.

Afterward, lead this discussion: **Why was it hard for Holly to forgive her brother? Describe a time you had trouble forgiving someone.** Share an example from your own life first.

Talk about: **When Holly's brother knocked her teeth out, she learned that God forgave her for free, so she needed to show that forgiveness to her brother. Because Jesus came to earth and died on the cross, it's possible for all of us to receive that same forgiveness—for free! We need to make sure we're always willing to forgive others.** *Anyone can be forgiven.*

PRAYER
Thank you, God, for sending Jesus to die for us, for forgiving us, and for listening to our prayers. In Jesus' name, amen.

TAKE-HOME PAGE

Give each child a Take-Home page. Encourage kids to select one of the six challenges for the week ahead.

YOU'LL NEED:

✓ *Grow Together Now* **DVD**
✓ **DVD player**

LESSON 4 | ANYONE CAN BE FORGIVEN

TAKE-HOME

PRACTICING FORGIVENESS

Keep growing in your faith and character. Choose one of the following challenges to do this week to acknowledge God's forgiveness in your life.

CHALLENGE 1
Find some good skipping rocks, and go to a body of water with an adult. Skip the rocks across the water and pray for forgiveness for a sin as you do. For each time the rock skips, thank Jesus for his forgiveness.

CHALLENGE 2
Show forgiveness to others. When family members or friends do things that hurt you, forgive them instead of getting angry. Remember that Jesus made it possible for you to receive forgiveness. Be like Jesus!

CHALLENGE 3
Mix food coloring in glue, and then use a craft stick to make the shape of a cross with the glue on wax paper. Let it dry, and then peel it off the wax paper. Give it to someone to hang in a window, and share with that person about Jesus' forgiveness.

  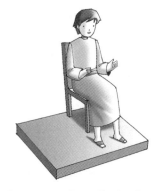

CHALLENGE 4
Read Acts 9:1-19 with your mom or dad before bed. As you read about Saul's conversion on the road to Damascus, think about the things you need to receive forgiveness for. Then ask Jesus to forgive you.

CHALLENGE 5
Using chalk, draw a picture of yourself on the sidewalk that shows how you feel when someone forgives you. Show your drawing to a family member, and tell him or her we receive forgiveness through Jesus.

CHALLENGE 6
Create a play about Saul with your friends who know how he met Jesus on the road to Damascus. Invite your neighborhood friends to watch it. Share with them that we receive forgiveness through Jesus like Saul did.

DEEDS WON'T DO

In this box, write a sin someone might commit.

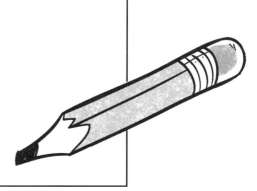

Write some good deeds people might do to get forgiveness on top of the sin you wrote in the box.

"God's love and forgiveness is like…"

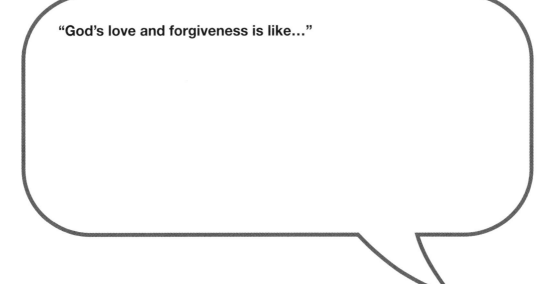

LESSON 4 | ANYONE CAN BE FORGIVEN

GOD HELPS US GET ALONG WITH OUR FAMILIES

LESSON 5

LEADER PREP

Genesis 13:1-18

LESSON AT A GLANCE

Abram was older, and he was the leader of his family, but he still gave Lot (his nephew) first choice of land. Abram gave up his first choice to keep peace in the family, and God rewarded him for it. Use this lesson to help children remember that God wants us to choose to get along with our families, even if it means giving up something.

PEACEMAKING IS... getting along with others.

WHAT KIDS DO	WHAT YOU'LL NEED
God Sightings *(5 minutes)* Talk about ways they've seen God at work.	
Explore the Bible! *(10 minutes)* Watch a video about two brothers deciding whether to get along.	• Bible • *Grow Together Now* DVD • DVD player
Getting Along *(15 minutes)* Consider ways that actions within their families affect their emotions.	• Bibles • copies of the handout *(found at the end of this lesson)* • crayons or markers • coins
Pattern for Love *(10 minutes)* Think about the pattern of getting along with their families.	• Bible • sheet of paper • coins from previous activity • marker
Got Coupons? *(10 minutes)* Create coupons for family members to get along.	• index cards • colored pencils
Live It! *(15 minutes)* Create skits about families getting along.	

*Photocopy the Take-Home page at the end of this lesson for each child.

ILLUSTRATED BY PAIGE BILLIN-FRYE

47

DEVOTIONS FOR LEADERS: PEACEMAKING

Sometimes the selfishness of others in our family makes it hard to live in harmony with them. It's very important that we strive to maintain healthy, harmonious relationships with the family God has given us. We need to be sure we don't contribute to any strife by our own actions. In the New Testament, Jesus—our ultimate example—said, "God blesses those who work for peace." Just as God blessed Abram for keeping the peace with Lot, he'll bless you for keeping the peace with your family members!

BIBLE BACKGROUND FOR LEADERS

Genesis 13:1-18: Abram and Lot Work Out Their Differences

SPENDING TIME IN EGYPT

Abram, who would later become known as Abraham, traveled south into Egypt because of a famine in the land of Canaan (Genesis 12:10). While in Egypt, Abram pretended to be Sarai's brother because Sarai was beautiful and he was afraid Pharaoh would kill him and take her. Pharaoh *did* have Sarai brought into his palace, but he treated Abram very well, giving him sheep, cattle, servants, and more. Abram became a very wealthy man during this time. In fact, this is the first time Abram is described as having silver and gold (Genesis 13:2). Then God began to inflict diseases on Pharaoh's household because Abram had lied. Sarai was Abram's wife, not his sister. When Pharaoh realized what had happened, he sent Abram and Sarai away. Abram and Lot headed back to the land God had promised to Abram's descendants.

A CONFLICT ARISES

In Genesis 13:5, we discover for the first time that Lot was wealthy as well. Yet it became apparent that Lot and Abram could no longer support both of their families' flocks and herds living close together. Conflicts between their herdsmen over land use could've easily become quarrels between Abram and Lot (Genesis 13:8).

ABRAM KEEPS THE PEACE

In this situation and culture, etiquette dictated that Lot allow Abram to take whatever he deemed was rightfully his because

ILLUSTRATED BY PAMELA JOHNSON

Abram was the respected elder and also more powerful and wealthy. The aged were to be cared for and treated with respect. So Abram's offer allowing Lot to choose which land he wanted probably shocked Lot—this was turning out far better than he'd hoped! Lot likely had fully expected to end up with the harshest, least fertile part of the land, but here was his chance to keep the fertile valley. Abram was willing to give up what was rightfully his to keep peace within his family. Lot, thinking only of himself, made a choice that his entire culture would've deemed unthinkable: He kept the good land for himself. The actions of these two men demonstrated the differences in their hearts.

GOD'S PROMISE

After Lot left, God spoke again to Abram, expanding on the promise made earlier and no doubt reaffirming to Abram that he'd done the right thing in keeping peace with Lot, even though for now he was stuck with inferior land. God commanded Abram to walk around his land. It was customary that a new landowner would walk the boundary of the land he was purchasing. God was telling Abram that he'd given Abram that land.

THE LESSON

GOD SIGHTINGS

Use the standard text provided or substitute your own examples for this weekly lesson-starter activity.

Say: **God is with us everywhere! When your friend shares with you, you feel God's kindness. When you smile at a stranger and hold open a door, you're being God at work. A beautiful sunset is evidence of God's creativity and power. It's important that we recognize and thank God for all the things he does in our lives. We call these God Sightings.**

Ask: **What evidence have you seen of God at work this week? Think about God's creation, ways people have encouraged you, and even ways God helped you make a difference for someone else.**

Share your own God Sighting first. Then let kids share God Sightings—evidence of God in our world. Then celebrate how God is at work in your lives through a prayer of thanksgiving.

YOU'LL NEED:

✓ Bible
✓ *Grow Together Now* DVD
✓ DVD player

EXPLORE THE BIBLE!

Talk about: **Even though we love our families, sometimes we get really, really mad at them. Raise your hand if you've ever been mad at someone in your family.** Pause for kids to raise their hands. **Yeah, me too! But you know what? Even during those times our families make us really mad, God still wants us to get along with them. Today we're going to learn that** *God helps us get along with our families.* **Even in Bible times, family members got mad at each other!**

Read aloud Genesis 13:1-18.

Say: **Abram and Lot had to work out their differences. We're going to watch a story now about two brothers who have to decide whether or not they will get along. Let's take a look.**

Show "Trouble at the Lab" (track 5) from the *Grow Together Now* DVD.

Lead this discussion: **What do you think about what these brothers did? Tell about a time you couldn't get along with someone in your family.** Share your own story first; then let kids share. **Why do we need to get along with our families?**

Talk about: **The brothers in the video were having a hard time getting along because neither one was willing to share with the other. In the Bible, it must've been really hard for Abram to give up the best land to his nephew Lot. But he did the right thing and gave up that land so he could get along with Lot. Abram knew that God wanted him to get along with his family. Abram also knew that God would help him do this, even though it was hard. We can only hope that the boys in our story made the right decision like Abram did. Just like Abram, we can trust that** *God helps us get along with our families.*

YOU'LL NEED:

✓ Bibles
✓ copies of the handout (found at the end of this lesson)
✓ crayons or markers
✓ coins

GETTING ALONG

Talk about: **Abram gave up the best land to his nephew, Lot. God was happy with Abram's choice, and he gave Abram even more land than he started with. Why do you think God rewarded Abram?**

Distribute handouts and writing and coloring supplies. Say: **Draw a picture of one way to get along with family. For example, you could draw a picture of sharing, hugging, or cleaning up toys.** Allow time.

Then continue: **Now find a partner and share about a recent time your family did something like the picture you drew.** Allow time.

Give each pair a Bible and two coins. Then say: **In your pairs, take turns tossing your coin onto the emojis on your handout. When the coin lands on a face, give a quick example of something a family member does that makes you feel that way.** Toss a coin onto a handout and share a quick example. If the coin lands on the angry face, you might say, "When my son leaves his dirty socks on the living room floor." Or if the coin lands on the sad face, you could say, "When my wife has a bad day at work." Let kids play for a few minutes.

Then have one person in each pair read aloud Romans 12:10. Gather kids and lead this discussion: **How do love and affection help your family straighten back out? Why is it hard to love your family when you feel negative emotions? How can you show that you rely on God to help you get along with your family?**

Say: **With God's help, you can straighten out any problems that are making your family feel mixed up right now.** *God helps us get along with our families.* **We don't try to do it on our own, because God helps us love better than we could by ourselves.**

PATTERN FOR LOVE

Say: **We learned that Abram gave up the best land to his nephew, Lot. God was happy with Abram's choice and gave Abram even more land than he started with.**

Have kids gather around your sheet of paper. Say: **One at a time, gently flip your coin onto the sheet of paper and leave it wherever it lands. Let's see if we can make a heart shape.**

Ask: **How easy or difficult was it to create a heart shape by flipping coins?**

YOU'LL NEED:

✓ **Bible**
✓ **sheet of paper**
✓ **coins from previous activity**
✓ **marker**

LESSON 5 | GOD HELPS US GET ALONG WITH OUR FAMILIES

Remove the coins, and use a marker to draw a large heart on the paper.

Say: **Now thoughtfully place your coin somewhere on the outside border of the heart as you say a silent prayer for God to help you get along with your family.**

Read aloud Romans 12:10 after all the coins have been placed.

Then lead this discussion: **Which was easier to do—flip a coin to make a heart shape, or carefully follow the pattern? How is the verse I read a pattern for getting along with your family?** (Read the verse again.) **What else would you add to this verse to get along with your family?**

Say: **Abram gave up his land to Lot, and God blessed him for doing that. When we choose to get along with our family members, God will bless us.** *God helps us get along with our families.*

GOT COUPONS?

Give each child a stack of cards, and have kids share colored pencils. Encourage them to create several coupons to help their family members get along with each other, such as give a hug, say something nice, share my toys, listen carefully, help dust, or do the dishes.

Say: **When you get home, invite your family members to make more coupons with their ideas using the blank cards. Then fold the cards, and put them in a bucket. Have each person pick out one card and then do the thing written on that card as often as possible throughout the day.**

When we do nice things for each other, we show God's love. *God helps us get along with our families.*

YOU'LL NEED:

✓ **index cards**
✓ **colored pencils**

LIVE IT!

Designate an area as the "stage."

Talk about: **Abram sacrificed what he wanted so he could keep a good relationship with Lot. God blessed Abram's generosity and gave him even more land than he started with. When we choose to get along with our families, God will bless us, too! Let's test our acting skills and create a skit about honoring our families.**

Have kids get into groups of three to six people, and instruct groups to spend a few minutes brainstorming a scene that shows a family choosing to get along. For example, they may choose to act out a family setting the dinner table together, going on a picnic, or sharing their TV time instead of fighting over it.

Allow time. Then have kids act out their skits "on stage."

Afterward, lead this discussion: **How was your skit like what happens in your own family? What happens when people don't get along in their families? What can you do to remember to get along with your family this week?**

Talk about: **It's not always easy to get along in families. Sometimes it means we have to give up what we want, stop ourselves from saying something we really want to, or even admit to being wrong. But easy or not, God wants us to get along with our families, and God will help us do it.** *God helps us get along with our families.*

PRAYER
Thank you, God, for loving each one of us and for giving us our families. Please help us get along with our families. In Jesus' name, amen.

TAKE-HOME PAGE

Give each child a Take-Home page. Encourage kids to select one of the six challenges for the week ahead.

FOR TEACHERS:
A LESSON FROM PENGUINS

Penguins in Antarctica rely on their families to survive. The parents spend many months of the year marching back and forth from the ocean to their breeding grounds to protect their eggs and find food for their babies. The penguins have to work together and get along to survive. It's the same with our families. When families work together and get along, they do much better.

LESSON 5 | GOD HELPS US GET ALONG WITH OUR FAMILIES

PRACTICING PEACEMAKING

Keep growing in your faith and character. Choose one of the following challenges to do this week to keep peace within your family.

CHALLENGE 1
Let your brother or sister choose a TV show or movie to watch, even if it's not your favorite.

CHALLENGE 2
Go on a bike ride with a friend. Take turns leading the way, while the person following shares one way he or she plans to get along better with a family member.

CHALLENGE 3
Ask every person in your family what you could do to get along better with everyone. Listen to what people have to say, and then try to do it this week.

CHALLENGE 4
Give at least one compliment to each person in your family (make sure you really mean it!). Keep track of the compliments you give in a notebook or journal, and add an emoticon showing the person's reaction after each compliment.

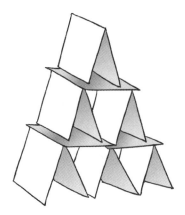

CHALLENGE 5
Ask a family member to help you make a building with playing cards. Talk about ways you can work on getting along.

CHALLENGE 6
Call an older family member you look up to, and ask about a time he or she had trouble getting along with someone. Find out what they did to make peace.

WE WORK TO GET ALONG

One way to get along with family:

LESSON 5 | GOD HELPS US GET ALONG WITH OUR FAMILIES

WE MAKE PEACE

LESSON 6

LEADER PREP

LESSON AT A GLANCE

Jacob had had enough. For 20 years he had been cheated and abused by his father-in-law, and it was time for a change. What's more, the Lord told Jacob it was time to go back to his homeland. So Jacob and his family packed up their things and left for Canaan. When his father-in-law, Laban, realized they had gone, he chased them down and accused Jacob of taking what belonged to him. In spite of his innocence, Jacob did what he could to settle his accounts with Laban and to part on peaceful terms. Use this lesson to help children settle accounts and make peace with the people around them.

Genesis 31:4-55

PEACEMAKING IS...
getting along with others.

WHAT KIDS DO	WHAT YOU'LL NEED
God Sightings *(5 minutes)* Talk about ways they've seen God at work.	
Explore the Bible! *(15 minutes)* Learn about the saga of Jacob and Laban.	• Bible
Walls & Bridges *(10 minutes)* Think about how we create walls between us and other people, and how that affects us.	• Bible • LEGO bricks or other building toys
Clay Peace *(10 minutes)* Consider how clay is like relationships.	• Bible • modeling clay • pencils
Compromise *(15 minutes)* Create skits to practice the art of compromising.	
Live It! *(15 minutes)* Name not-peaceful places in their lives.	• paper • chalk

*Photocopy the Take-Home page at the end of this lesson for each child.

ILLUSTRATED BY RONNIE ROONEY

57

DEVOTIONS FOR LEADERS: PEACEMAKING

Every day you encounter opportunities to be a peacemaker. And each time those opportunities come, God is there to help you through them. Perhaps he helps you hold your tongue when someone talks behind your back or helps you see a difficult situation from a different perspective. Watch for opportunities to be a peacemaker today. When those moments come, listen. See if God whispers something to you about being a peacemaker.

BIBLE BACKGROUND FOR LEADERS

Genesis 31:4-55: Laban Pursues Jacob

FAMILY FEUD

Jacob had two wives, Rachel and Leah. Their father, Laban, employed Jacob to tend his flock, but he cheated Jacob every possible way by changing the rules of payment time and again (Genesis 31:7). In spite of Laban's efforts, Jacob grew wealthy (Genesis 30:43). Then an angel came to Jacob in a dream and told him to leave. Jacob gathered his family and possessions and did as the angel said. When Laban found out, he pursued and caught up with Jacob. Jacob and Laban discussed their disagreements. Together, they and their families stacked rocks to represent a boundary line. They promised that they'd never cross it with the intent of harming each other.

GOD BRINGS PEACE

God had watched and protected Jacob during his 20 years of employment with Laban. God even changed the spots on newborn goats so Laban's schemes to cheat Jacob would fail. Injustice isn't something God approves of, but neither is revenge. So Jacob honored God by working hard the entire time. In the end, God helped inspire a peaceful outcome rather than a family feud between Jacob and Laban. Jacob made peace—even with a man who'd manipulated him for 20 years.

MODELING GOD'S PEACE

God encourages us to be peacemakers like Jacob. Jesus said, "Blessed are the peacemakers, for they will be called sons of God" (Matthew 5:9). True, when we face conflict it's easier to withdraw to a safe spot and settle for talking *about* people rather than talking *with* them. Then no one misunderstands us or turns their anger our direction. But that's not peacemaking. God uses peacemakers—like us—to enter places thick with conflict, to reflect his values and model his peace.

THE LESSON

GOD SIGHTINGS

Use the standard text provided or substitute your own examples for this weekly lesson-starter activity.

Say: **God is with us everywhere! When your friend shares with you, you feel God's kindness. When you smile at a stranger and hold open a door, you're being God at work. A beautiful sunset is evidence of God's creativity and power. It's important that we recognize and thank God for all the things he does in our lives. We call these God Sightings.**

Ask: **What evidence have you seen of God at work this week? Think about God's creation, ways people have encouraged you, and even ways God helped you make a difference for someone else.**

Share your own God Sighting first. Then let kids share God Sightings—evidence of God in our world. Then celebrate how God is at work in your lives through a prayer of thanksgiving.

EXPLORE THE BIBLE!

Talk about: **Today we'll talk about making peace. Listen and think of ways someone could make peace in this squabble.**

Read Genesis 31:4-9. Say: **Jacob worked for Laban as a shepherd for many years. Despite Laban's dishonesty, Jacob became rich and successful, making Laban jealous. And though Jacob became rich, he still felt cheated.**

Lead this discussion: **What are some ways Jacob and Laban could have made peace in this situation? Tell about a time you made peace, even though you didn't feel you were wrong.** Give an example from your own life; then let kids share.

YOU'LL NEED:

✓ **Bible**

LESSON 6 | WE MAKE PEACE

Paraphrase Genesis 31:10-21: **Jacob dreamed God told him to pack up everything and return to his homeland. Rachel and Leah agreed to go along because they were unhappy with their father, Laban, too. In fact, Rachel even stole her father's household idols as they were leaving. Not even Jacob knew she stole things.**

Lead this discussion: **Explain whether you think leaving Laban was a good way for Jacob to make peace. Was it okay for Rachel to take something from her father's home since he was unfair to her? Why or why not?**

Read Genesis 31:22-32. Then say: **Laban chased Jacob and found him. Laban was angry. And Rachel had hid the household idols in her camel saddle and was sitting on them. Laban rummaged through their belongings but couldn't find them anywhere. Jacob was angry that Laban accused him of stealing.**

Lead this discussion: **What could Jacob have done to make peace now?**

Read Genesis 31:38-55, which starts with Jacob's response. Talk about: **Jacob finally stood up to Laban. Then they made peace by promising never to set foot on each other's land again.**

Lead this discussion: **What was good or bad about Jacob standing up to Laban? Explain if you think it's ever okay to end a friendship in order to keep peace.**

Talk about: **Running away from problems usually doesn't solve them or make peace. But doing what God wants you to do is always right.** *We make peace*, **just as Jacob did.**

WALLS & BRIDGES

Gather kids around a large pile of LEGO bricks or other building toys.

Say: **Jacob lived with and worked for Laban for 20 years. Laban's treatment of Jacob caused bad feelings.**

Have kids use the bricks to construct a wall. Then lead this discussion: **What kinds of things do walls do? What kinds of things create walls or division between friends?**

YOU'LL NEED:

✓ **Bible**
✓ **LEGO bricks or other building toys**

Say: **When others hurt us or mistreat us, we build walls to protect ourselves. They're not walls like this brick one or ones around a building. They're walls of silence or awkwardness. Those walls stop us from being close with others—from having peaceful, loving relationships.**

Ask: **When has a wall been built between you and someone else? How did you handle it?** Give an example from your own life first to get kids thinking.

Say: **The Bible tells us what breaks down those walls between people.** Read Ephesians 2:13-15, explaining that the Jews and Gentiles believed different things about God and how to worship him. Have kids knock down the wall they've built. Then lead this discussion: **What can you learn from these verses about knocking down walls? What can you do to knock down a wall that has been built between you and someone else?**

Gather kids around the building toys again. This time ask them to build a bridge. Say: **Think of someone you have a lot in common with, like your brother or sister or a best friend. As you work on the bridge, tell a partner about something you have in common with the person you thought of.** Allow time.

As kids continue to work on the bridge, ask them to think about these questions:

- **What are some things you have in common with someone you don't get along with?**
- **How can you use those things to make peace with that person?**

Say: **When we focus on how we're alike,** *we can make peace in our relationships.*

CLAY PEACE

Say: **Jacob spent a lot of time and effort trying to get along with Laban. He worked hard for Laban, he respected Laban's property, and he even made personal sacrifices when he didn't need to. But Laban still treated Jacob badly.**

**Sometimes we face situations where we just can't make peace because the other person doesn't want to. But no

YOU'LL NEED:

✓ **Bible**
✓ **modeling clay**
✓ **pencils**

matter what, we can do our part in peacemaking. And you never know when a change will come. It took a lot of problems to tear apart Jacob and Laban's relationship, but just one conversation, led by God, helped them make peace. *We make peace* with others no matter what it takes. Here's something else the Bible tells us about peace.

Read aloud Romans 12:18.

Distribute modeling clay and pencils, and say: **Think about someone you just can't get along with, no matter how hard you try. Work with your clay as you think about all the reasons you're upset with that person. Create a face with your clay, and use your pencil to make an expression of how it feels to not be at peace with this person.** Allow time.

Now, roll up that face and sculpt a standing cross as you think about reasons you like the person you're upset with.

Talk about: **How is working with modeling clay like working on relationships with other people?**

Say: **When we're fighting with someone, it tears apart our relationship and takes a lot of our energy. God's desire is for everyone to live at peace. When we're not living in peace with others, it's hard for us to be at peace with God.**

COMPROMISE

Form two groups, and number them 1 and 2.

Talk about what it means to compromise. Then read each of the situations below, and have each group represent one of the sides in the disagreement. Ask the groups to find a peaceful solution by finding a way to compromise.

- **Group 1 will represent a brother who wants to spend the afternoon playing soccer at the park. Group 2 will be a sister who wants to spend the afternoon playing dolls at home. Your mom says you must stay together.**

- **Groups 1 and 2 are science partners, and you have to decide on a project. Group 1 wants to do something on bugs, but Group 2 wants to make a volcano.**

- **Groups 1 and 2 both want to watch their favorite shows, but they're different shows. The shows are on at the same time, and there's only one television.**

Have group members each tell about a time they had to make a compromise. Talk about: **What was it like to compromise? How did compromising help in making peace in your situation?**

Say: **When we compromise,** *we make peace.*

LIVE IT!

Give each child paper and a piece of chalk.

Say: **Trace around your hand with the chalk. Then, in the outline of your hand, use the chalk to draw pictures or write words that remind you of places or situations in your life that cause you not to feel peaceful. You might write "bully" if someone bullies you. Or you might write "sister" if you aren't getting along with her.**

Allow time, and then say: **Maybe you can't help with a bully or a sick grandmother, but you can pray for each other. Put your hand picture and a partner's hand picture together like praying hands. Take turns rubbing the papers together as you pray for your partner.** Allow time for prayer. Then have kids look at their hand pictures and notice that their words and drawings are smeared.

Lead this discussion: **How can prayer help smooth out the things in your life that lack peace?**

Talk about: **God won't always take away the things in our lives that lack peace. He didn't take away Jacob's bad relationship with Laban. But he did help smooth things out, just as the chalk on our hand pictures smoothed out so you can't really read the words.** *We make peace* **with God's help.**

PRAYER

Thank you, God, that you help us make peace. Help us not to run away from our problems but to quickly make peace by praying about the things in our lives that lack peace and by always showing your love. In Jesus' name, amen.

TAKE-HOME PAGE

Give each child a Take-Home page. Encourage kids to select one of the six challenges for the week ahead.

YOU'LL NEED:

✓ **paper**
✓ **chalk**

LEADER TIP

Play age-appropriate music quietly in the background while kids work.

LESSON 6 | WE MAKE PEACE

TAKE-HOME

PRACTICING PEACEMAKING

Keep growing in your faith and character. Choose one of the following challenges to do this week to grow in making peace.

CHALLENGE 1
Read Galatians 6:10. Think of one good thing you can do today for someone you're having a hard time getting along with. Then do it!

CHALLENGE 2
Go for a walk and find several small stones that will stack on top of each other. Use those stones to create a small pillar in a place you will see often, like a dresser or table in your bedroom. When you're at odds with someone, look at your stone pillar as a reminder to make peace, just as Jacob and Laban did.

CHALLENGE 3
Sometimes we're the ones primarily responsible for the lack of peace in our relationships. Think of someone you are at odds with because of something you did. Go to that person and ask for forgiveness to begin rebuilding the relationship.

CHALLENGE 4
Read Luke 6:27-28. Then look for ways to put those verses into practice today.

CHALLENGE 5
Think of someone you're having a hard time getting along with, and look for something you have in common. Create something if necessary: Invite the person to a group activity you think might interest him or her, or learn about something you know is an interest to that person. Then use that thing you now share in common to begin establishing a new connection with that person.

CHALLENGE 6
Put some potting soil into a paper cup, and plant a flower seed in the soil. Then place the cup in a window and water it. Write out the words to James 3:18 on a piece of paper and tape it to the side of the cup as a reminder to sow peace in all your relationships today. Read the verse as a reminder each time you water your seed.

WE PRAY WHEN PEOPLE ARE MEAN

LESSON 7

LEADER PREP

Nehemiah 4:1-9

LESSON AT A GLANCE
God led Nehemiah to rebuild the walls of Jerusalem. Nehemiah guided the workers night and day, even while their enemies mocked and threatened them. Instead of retaliating, Nehemiah prayed, trusting that God would protect his people and show Nehemiah what to do. Use this lesson to help children learn to pray for people when they're mean.

PEACEMAKING IS...
getting along with others.

WHAT KIDS DO	WHAT YOU'LL NEED
God Sightings *(5 minutes)* Talk about ways they've seen God at work.	
Explore the Bible! *(10 minutes)* Use drawings to explore the Bible passage.	• Bible • paper • chalk
Bully Ball *(10 minutes)* Create a shield to protect their spinning coins from the tennis ball "bully."	• Bible • coins • tennis ball
It's Puzzling *(10 minutes)* Consider how prayer can put relationships back together like a puzzle.	• copies of the handout *(found at the end of this lesson)* on card stock • colored pencils • scissors • sandwich bags
Popcorn Story *(10 minutes)* Create a group story about praying when people are mean.	
Live It! *(10 minutes)* Watch a video about a colony of ants.	• *Grow Together Now* DVD • DVD player

ILLUSTRATED BY PAIGE BILLIN-FRYE

*Photocopy the Take-Home page at the end of this lesson for each child.

DEVOTIONS FOR LEADERS: PEACEMAKING

When we're doing God's work, we often face opposition, skepticism, even persecution. Under these circumstances, what do we do? Despair? Throw in the towel? Nehemiah prayed. We can, too. But remember: God's answers always involve our obedience. Are you facing great odds? Are people ridiculing your faithfulness? Take a lesson from Nehemiah. Train your eyes on God. Pray. Obey. And don't ever, ever give up.

BIBLE BACKGROUND FOR LEADERS

Nehemiah 4:1-9: Enemies Threaten Nehemiah

FROM NAY TO PRAY

When we attempt something great for God, there'll always be those who say we can't do it. Sanballat the Samarian and Tobiah the Ammonite were two such naysayers. They mocked Nehemiah and his workers for thinking they were capable of rebuilding the wall around Jerusalem. After all, these Israelites were unskilled; their plans were unrealistic. In fact, in Nehemiah 4:10, the people of Judah started to believe the naysayers and began complaining that the task was too difficult.

LOOK WHO'S MOCKING

ILLUSTRATED BY DREW ROSE

Against such odds, it wouldn't have been surprising if Nehemiah had given up. But he didn't. Instead, he prayed. He took his concerns to God. Nehemiah realized that his enemies weren't mocking him; they were mocking God. Even though God's people were doing the work, Nehemiah understood what the psalmist said: "Unless the Lord builds a house, the work of the builders is wasted" (Psalm 127:1). God desired for the Jewish people to rebuild the walls around Jerusalem, so really it was God's name on the line. However, Nehemiah also clearly understood his responsibility as an obedient follower of God. God wanted Nehemiah to stand up to his adversaries, namely Sanballat and Tobiah.

PRAYER PARTICIPATION

St. Augustine, Catholic saint and an important historical figure in the development of Christianity, is quoted as having said: "Do what you can, and then pray that God will give you the power to do what you cannot." In other words, God wants us to participate with him in the answering of our prayers. In Nehemiah 4:9, the people "prayed to our God and guarded the city." God never intended prayer to be a passive activity. Prayer and action go hand in hand. For Nehemiah, praying to God also meant guarding the wall.

THE LESSON

GOD SIGHTINGS

Use the standard text provided or substitute your own examples for this weekly lesson-starter activity.

Say: **God is with us everywhere! When your friend shares with you, you feel God's kindness. When you smile at a stranger and hold open a door, you're being God at work. A beautiful sunset is evidence of God's creativity and power. It's important that we recognize and thank God for all the things he does in our lives. We call these God Sightings.**

Ask: **What evidence have you seen of God at work this week? Think about God's creation, ways people have encouraged you, and even ways God helped you make a difference for someone else.**

Share your own God Sighting first. Then let kids share God Sightings—evidence of God in our world. Then celebrate how God is at work in your lives through a prayer of thanksgiving.

EXPLORE THE BIBLE!

Hand out pieces of paper and chalk.

Talk about: **The Bible tells us about a guy named Nehemiah who loved God. Nehemiah worked for a king and heard bad news about his hometown. The wall around Jerusalem was smashed to pieces! Nehemiah felt he was supposed to rebuild the wall. But when Nehemiah started rebuilding the wall, men named Sanballat and Tobiah started making fun of his work. Nehemiah used burned-out bricks and materials to rebuild the walls, and Sanballat thought this was silly.**

YOU'LL NEED:

✓ **Bible**
✓ **paper**
✓ **chalk**

Have kids fold the pieces of paper in half like a book. Say: **Let's hear what happened next.** Read Nehemiah 4:1-3.

Then say: **Think about a time someone was mean to you, the way Sanballat and Tobiah were mean to Nehemiah. Draw that experience on the front of your "book."** Allow time; then continue the Bible story.

Read Nehemiah 4:4-5. Have kids draw themselves praying on the second page of their books.

Read Nehemiah 4:6-8. On the back page of their books, have kids draw Sanballat and Tobiah, angry at the wall.

Read Nehemiah 4:9. On the third page of their books, have kids draw Nehemiah praying.

Have kids place their books on the floor, like a tent, so both pictures of people being mean are face-up. **When people hurt or make fun of us...** (demonstrate how to flip the papers over so the praying pictures are showing) **we can pray! Just like Nehemiah, we can flip things around just by praying!**

Lead this discussion: **When people are mean, how are you like or unlike Nehemiah? How does prayer "flip" things around?**

Talk about: **Nobody likes to be laughed at. Like Nehemiah,** *we pray when people are mean.*

BULLY BALL

Say: **Some people in the Bible were mean to Nehemiah. They wanted to knock down his spirit and stop him from obeying God. Let's play a game to see what that's like in our lives.**

Gather kids around a table, and demonstrate how to spin a coin by holding it on its edge and giving it a flick with your finger. This will take some practice. See who can make the coins spin longest.

As kids are spinning their coins, start rolling a tennis ball on the table in an attempt to knock over coins. Do this several times.

YOU'LL NEED:

- ✓ **Bible**
- ✓ **coins**
- ✓ **tennis ball**

Then lead this discussion: **How was the tennis ball like a bully to the spinning coins? How could you protect your coin from the bully? How do you protect yourself from bullies? How could prayer make a difference when bullies treat you unkindly?**

Say: *We pray when people are mean* **to us, and when we pray, God helps us know how to react or when to walk away. Sometimes God will comfort us. God may also use our prayers to help mean people change what they're doing. Another guy in the Bible was named David, and he knew a thing or two about bullies. Listen to what David wrote in the Bible.**

Read aloud Psalm 33:20.

Let kids use anything in the classroom to create a shield to protect their spinning coins. Roll the tennis ball again, and let kids protect their coins.

Lead this discussion: **How well did your shield protect the coins? What makes God a better protector than anything?**

Say: **God is a strong shield, and we can depend on him to protect us because he's more powerful than anything that could hurt or scare us. That's why** *we pray when people are mean.*

IT'S PUZZLING

Distribute bags of puzzle pieces (see Leader Prep) and colored pencils. Have kids pair up if you have younger kids who may need help from older kids.

Say: **When bullies were mean to Nehemiah, he led his people and prayed to God. Fill out your puzzle piece about someone you know who reacts well when people are mean. Just write that person's name.** Allow time.

What's most puzzling about why people bully others? Why do people say and do mean things? Find that puzzle piece and write your response. Allow time and then discuss.

YOU'LL NEED:

✓ **copies of the handout** *(found at the end of this lesson)* **on card stock**

✓ **colored pencils**

✓ **scissors**

✓ **sandwich bags**

LEADER PREP

Copy the handouts onto card stock. Then cut apart each puzzle and put the pieces in a sandwich bag. You'll need one bag per person.

LESSON 7 | WE PRAY WHEN PEOPLE ARE MEAN

Next piece: How does bullying hurt friendships? Allow time and then discuss.

What happens if you're mean back when someone is mean to you? Allow time and then discuss.

Have you ever faced a bully? What happened? Find the puzzle piece and write or draw about that. Allow time and then discuss.

How does prayer help when people are mean? There's a piece for that. Allow time and then discuss.

Next, think about what would help you remember to pray first when people are mean to you. Fill out that piece. Allow time and then discuss.

Talk about: **On your last piece, write what you should do when prayer isn't enough. Let's share ideas as you write or draw.**

As kids put their puzzles together, say: **When people are mean to us and we're mean back, tempers flare and a situation can get really crazy and messy. But prayer can help us put relationships back together, like a puzzle.**

Nehemiah trusted God and prayed when enemies came. Whenever you see people doing mean things, remember that *we pray when people are mean.*

POPCORN STORY

Gather everyone in a circle and tell a "popcorn story" together.

Give these instructions: **For a popcorn story, one person starts a story by jumping up, saying one sentence, and then sitting back down. Then the next person adds a sentence to the story in the same manner, and so on.**

Start a story about a preschooler who gets picked on. For example: **Once there was a boy named Sue, and all the kids at his preschool made fun of him because they said Sue was a girl's name.**

Take turns adding one sentence at a time to the story.

Lead the story to a happy ending. Afterward, lead this discussion: **How did the characters in the story respond to people being mean? How can family members respond when people are mean to them?**

Say: **Instead of responding back in a mean way,** *we pray when people are mean.*

LIVE IT!

Talk about: **While Nehemiah was fixing the broken wall around Jerusalem, people started making fun of him and of his work. Let's imagine that close by, a colony of ants was going through the same thing. Take a look.**

Show "The Wall" (track 6) from the *Grow Together Now* DVD.

Afterward, lead this discussion: **What did you think about what Tobiah and Sanballat said to the ants? How would you have responded?**

Talk about: **The way we react to things is so important! Our first instinct might be to make fun, to try to argue, or to fight back. Nehemiah chose to pray when Sanballat and Tobiah started making fun. We can react in the same way—because** *we pray when people are mean.*

PRAYER
Thank you, God, for listening to us when we pray, protecting us from hurtful words and actions, and teaching us how to deal with people who are mean to us. In Jesus' name, amen.

TAKE-HOME PAGE

Give each child a Take-Home page. Encourage kids to select one of the six challenges for the week ahead.

YOU'LL NEED:

✓ *Grow Together Now* **DVD**

✓ **DVD player**

FOR TEACHERS:
INVITING PEACE

Children—no matter the age—often won't have the maturity to bring peace into a situation themselves. Look for opportunities where children are dealing with a conflict that isn't resolving. Use that opportunity to shape their character by pointing out that sometimes the best way to bring peace to a situation is to ask someone else to help. Then let them know you're available to help.

TAKE-HOME

PRACTICING PEACEMAKING

Keep growing in your faith and character. Choose one of the following challenges to do this week to pray when people are mean.

CHALLENGE 1

Write on pieces of paper the names of people who have been mean to you. Place the papers in a container by your bed. Throughout the day, choose one name, ask God to comfort any hurt feelings you have, and then pray for that person.

CHALLENGE 2

Ask your parent to take you to the park. Bring three small gifts, such as pieces of candy or pencils with cool designs. Be on the lookout for three people being treated poorly. Give them each one of your presents as a way to cheer them up. Then pray for them and for the people who were mean to them.

CHALLENGE 3

When people are mean to us, it's like getting stuck with something sharp. Pin a safety pin to your jacket or its zipper. Every time you see someone being mean, touch the pin and pray, asking God to heal the wounds the mean person caused and to help that person be more kind.

CHALLENGE 4

Find an old key, or draw one on paper or cardboard, and write the word "pray" on it. Put it on a necklace or bracelet, or just keep it with you as a reminder that praying is the key to situations where people are mean.

CHALLENGE 5

Read Nehemiah 4:1-9 in your Bible. Then, in a notebook or journal, rewrite the passage as if it were happening today. Instead of building a wall, what might people who follow God be doing? Who might be mean to them, and what could those people do? How could the people following God respond? Then pray and ask God to guide you whenever you see people being mean.

CHALLENGE 6

Draw a brick wall. See if you can fill each brick with a prayer for someone you see being mean or someone who has to deal with mean people. Build your wall of prayer as Nehemiah did.

HANDOUT

Someone who reacts well when people are mean:

If I'm mean back...

What's most puzzling about why people bully others?

How prayer helps when people are mean:

How I can remember to pray first:

How does bullying hurt friendships?

When prayer isn't enough, I should...

A time I faced a bully:

LESSON 7 | WE PRAY WHEN PEOPLE ARE MEAN

GOD GIVES US PEACE

LESSON 8

LEADER PREP

LESSON AT A GLANCE
Jesus told his disciples not to worry about what they would eat, drink, or wear. He reminded them that God feeds the birds and dresses the flowers, and God will take care of us. In Galatians, Paul reminds us that peace is a fruit of the Spirit. Use this lesson to help children learn that when we believe in God and trust him, God will help us have peace.

Matthew 6:25-34

PEACEMAKING IS...
getting along with others.

WHAT KIDS DO	WHAT YOU'LL NEED
God Sightings *(5 minutes)* Talk about ways they've seen God at work.	
Explore the Bible! *(10 minutes)* Experience relaxing and focusing on God.	• Bible
Bird Mobile *(15 minutes)* Make flocks of birds to remind them that God takes care of them.	• strips of paper • hangers • stapler • string or yarn • pencils
Peace Stones *(10 minutes)* Create a peace stone to remind them that God gives us peace.	• Bible • flat stones • permanent markers • pens or pencils
Popping Worries *(10 minutes)* Talk about worries as they pop popcorn.	• bags of microwave popcorn • microwave • napkins
Live It! *(10 minutes)* Watch a video about a frustrating situation.	• *Grow Together Now* DVD • DVD player

*Photocopy the Take-Home page at the end of this lesson for each child.

ILLUSTRATED BY PAIGE BILLIN-FRYE

DEVOTIONS FOR LEADERS: PEACEMAKING

Peace isn't one of those things you can manufacture. Real peace is more than a bandage over worry or a calm façade that cracks at the first sign of trouble. Real peace must be preceded by radical trust. Try it—try to do exactly what Jesus challenges in Matthew 6. With his help, transform your feelings of stress and worry over bills, work, lists, and responsibilities. In prayer, give them to God. Name your anxieties one by one. Affirm your belief in God's provision and guidance. Rely on him to help you. Remember that God already knows all your needs. How will you trust him more fully today?

BIBLE BACKGROUND FOR LEADERS

Matthew 6:25-34: Jesus Teaches About Peace

NO SHOES, NO SHIRT, NO FOOD?

Among Jesus' many radical teachings in the Gospels is this challenge: "I tell you not to worry about everyday life—whether you have enough food and drink, or enough clothes to wear." This may be one of the most counterintuitive calls we receive. Don't plan? Don't scramble? Don't self-protect? Don't focus all sorts of anxiety and effort on the basics of survival? God feeds the birds and clothes the flowers, Jesus explains, so don't worry.

HAND 'EM OVER

Jesus is not elevating adolescent irresponsibility to spiritual-discipline level. His call to "not worry" doesn't add up to a "problem-free philosophy." Instead, Jesus challenges us to surrender completely to God and rely on him for provision. Jesus says that, rather than stressing about details, we can put our focus on seeking "the kingdom of God above all else."

SO WHERE'S THE PEACE?

Jesus doesn't explicitly mention "peace" in Matthew 6:25-34, so what does this passage have to do with peace? First, consider our understanding of what "peace" itself is. It's not merely the absence of conflict; it's something much deeper. In this passage, Jesus explains the foundation upon which inner peace rests: trust in God. When we rely fully on God, we can "experience God's peace, which

ILLUSTRATED BY PAMELA JOHNSON

exceeds anything we can understand" (Philippians 4:7). This logic-defying peace is a gift given by God through the Holy Spirit.

INNER PEACE, OUTER PEACE

It's tough to fully trust God sometimes—that's why we need the Spirit's help, enabling us to relinquish our desire for control and power. As we grow in the Spirit and experience the peace that comes from trusting God, we also grow in our ability to extend that peace to others. Peace is one of many harvest fruits the Holy Spirit produces in our lives. Through God's power, we also live lives characterized by love, joy, patience, kindness, goodness, faithfulness, gentleness, and self-control (Galatians 5:22-23).

THE LESSON

GOD SIGHTINGS

Use the standard text provided or substitute your own examples for this weekly lesson-starter activity.

Say: **God is with us everywhere! When your friend shares with you, you feel God's kindness. When you smile at a stranger and hold open a door, you're being God at work. A beautiful sunset is evidence of God's creativity and power. It's important that we recognize and thank God for all the things he does in our lives. We call these God Sightings.**

Ask: **What evidence have you seen of God at work this week? Think about God's creation, ways people have encouraged you, and even ways God helped you make a difference for someone else.**

Share your own God Sighting first. Then let kids share God Sightings—evidence of God in our world. Then celebrate how God is at work in your lives through a prayer of thanksgiving.

LESSON 8 | GOD GIVES US PEACE

YOU'LL NEED:

✓ **Bible**

EXPLORE THE BIBLE!

Ask kids to each think about something they often worry about (or are worried about right now). Have them strike a worried pose and tense all their muscles. Then tell them to let it go.

Say: **Jesus says we worry when we don't need to! Let's listen to Jesus and try this again. When I say "go," get into your worried pose again and keep all your muscles tight! I'll tell you when you can relax. Ready? Go!**

Read aloud Matthew 6:25-27. Say: **Okay, you can relax your face and neck muscles now (but only those muscles!)— Jesus tells us he'll take care of us.**

Read aloud verses 28 to 30. Say: **You can relax your arms and hands now—Jesus tells us he'll provide us with the things we need.**

Read aloud verses 31 and 32. Say: **You can relax your legs and lie down now—Jesus tells us to trust him because he knows what we need.**

Read aloud verses 33 and 34. Say: **Close your eyes and take a deep breath. Jesus tells us not to worry but instead to focus on living for him—and he'll take care of all of those other things for us.**

Lead this discussion: **Explain which you like better: being worried or being relaxed. Tell about something God has taken care of that you worried about. Tell about something you need to trust God for right now.** Give your own examples for the last two questions; then let kids share.

Talk about: **We're more important to God than the flowers and birds. He takes care of them, so he must want to take care of us, too! The Bible reminds us that *God gives us peace*. God will take care of us. All we have to do is trust him.**

BIRD MOBILE

Say: **Jesus told his friends not to worry about what they would eat or drink or wear. Jesus reminded his friends that God feeds the birds and dresses the flowers.**

Tell a partner about what you do when you worry. Allow time. Then invite participants to share with the group.

Gather kids around the supplies. **In small lettering, write one of your worries on a corner of a strip of paper. Now make flocks of birds to help you remember that you don't need to worry about these things because God gives us peace.**

Give these instructions:

1. **Fold each strip so the sides form a 90-degree angle** (see illustration)**.**
2. **Draw a bird face and feathers on the birds.**
3. **Staple one end of a piece of string or yarn to each bird. Tie the other end to a hanger.**
4. **Use different lengths of string so the birds hang at different heights.**

Lead this discussion: **Why do you think God doesn't want us to worry about things? What are some ways God takes care of you?**

Say: **We all worry sometimes, but God wants us to trust him instead of worrying. Like the birds and flowers, we're in God's hands, and we know that God will take care of us. The next time you start to worry about something, remember that** *God gives us peace.*

YOU'LL NEED:

✓ **strips of paper**
✓ **hangers**
✓ **stapler**
✓ **string or yarn**
✓ **pencils**

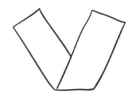

LESSON 8 | GOD GIVES US PEACE

PEACE STONES

YOU'LL NEED:

- ✓ Bible
- ✓ flat stones
- ✓ permanent markers
- ✓ pens or pencils

Say: **Today we're learning not to worry about what we eat or drink or wear. Just as God takes care of the birds and the flowers, God will take care of us.**

Read aloud Matthew 6:25-29.

Say: **Some people carry around small stones called worry stones. Often, people rub worry stones to feel calmer. Today we'll each make our own worry stone, but we'll call it a peace stone to remember that we can turn to God when we're worried and he'll give us peace. You may want to draw a bird, a smiley face, or a flower.**

Gather kids around the supplies, and let them create. Afterward, lead this discussion: **How does knowing that God takes care of birds and flowers give you peace? What will you do now when you're worried about something?**

Read aloud Philippians 4:6-7. Talk about: **How can the truth in these verses help you when you're worried?**

Say: **When you start to worry about things in your life, remember: God takes care of birds and flowers, and you're much more important to God. That's why *God gives us peace.***

POPPING WORRIES

YOU'LL NEED:

- ✓ bags of microwave popcorn
- ✓ microwave
- ✓ napkins

ALLERGY ALERT

Consult with parents and be aware of any allergies the kids in your group might have.

Gather kids around a microwave, where you'll pop several bags of popcorn, one bag at a time.

Share things you're each worried about as the popcorn pops.

Notice how the popping calms down as the process is complete. Talk about: **What does it feel like to have worries bouncing around inside of us, quickly pop-pop-popping in our minds? How does that compare to when we let *God give us peace?***

Enjoy the popcorn together.

LIVE IT!

Talk about: **Every morning, some people stand in front of their closet and face a choice: what...to...wear. It can ruin their mood for the whole day if they're wearing something that doesn't fit right. They get so worried about what they're going to wear! If you can relate to that, you can relate to this video. Let's check it out.**

Show "You Choose" (track 7) from the *Grow Together Now* DVD.

Afterward, lead this discussion: **What was different between the two ways the girl reacted to situations? How do you think reading the Bible helped the girl during the day? What can you do to have God's peace when dealing with worrisome things?**

Talk about: **Reading her Bible didn't automatically give the girl a problem-free day, but it did help her handle those problems in a more peaceful way. Frustrating and difficult things will happen, but how we react to those things is up to us! If we spend time with God, we'll find that** *God gives us peace.*

PRAYER
Thank you, God, for taking care of us, down to the smallest detail. Please show us a peace that passes all understanding, even in times of trouble. In Jesus' name, amen.

TAKE-HOME PAGE

Give each child a Take-Home page. Encourage kids to select one of the six challenges for the week ahead.

YOU'LL NEED:

✓ ***Grow Together Now* DVD**
✓ **DVD player**

FOR TEACHERS:
DON'T WORRY

Worry is prayer turned inward. When we worry, we're looking to ourselves for a solution to what bothers us. Teach your children instead to take their concerns to God in outward prayer.

LESSON 8 | GOD GIVES US PEACE

TAKE-HOME

PRACTICING PEACEMAKING

Keep growing in your faith and character. Choose one of the following challenges to do this week to remember that God gives us peace.

CHALLENGE 1
Read Galatians 5:22-23. Then draw a picture of a piece of fruit, and put it where you'll see it every day. If you start to worry, look at your picture and remember that when you believe in God and trust him, you can have the fruit of the Spirit, peace, because you know he'll take care of you.

CHALLENGE 2
Look for someone who is worried about something. Share with that person what Jesus said about not worrying and how God gives us peace.

CHALLENGE 3
Look at nature in a new way. Every time you see a bird or flower, remember Jesus' words about not worrying.

CHALLENGE 4
Using paint or markers, make a peace stone with a friend who has seemed worried lately. Tell your friend how the peace stone reminds you that you don't have to worry because you can have peace through God.

CHALLENGE 5
With your parents' permission, go online and find simple instructions for making an origami bird. Once you've figured out how to make the bird, teach a friend. Then tell your friend what you learned about how we can have peace because God takes care of the birds and us.

CHALLENGE 6
Make a list of worries you have right now. Spend time praying, asking God to give you peace in each situation. Then tear up the list and commit to praying to God to give you peace whenever you're faced with worries.

WE BRING PEACE

LESSON 9

Philemon 1:4-22

PEACEMAKING IS...
getting along with others.

LEADER PREP

LESSON AT A GLANCE

Paul faced a difficult situation. Two of his friends and fellow believers were at odds and needed someone to bring peace to the situation. So Paul got involved. He wrote a letter asking the offended party to see the situation through eyes of love, to forgive the other person, and to accept him as a brother in Christ. Use this lesson to help children bring peace to the conflicts around them.

WHAT KIDS DO	WHAT YOU'LL NEED
God Sightings *(5 minutes)* Talk about ways they've seen God at work.	
Explore the Bible! *(10 minutes)* Write a letter to Paul and Onesimus.	• Bibles • paper • pencils
Stand By Clay *(15 minutes)* Consider how other people's stories might affect the entire situation.	• Bible • modeling clay
Dog-Eared *(10 minutes)* Consider whether they should get involved in conflicts.	• Bible • paper • pencils
Peacemaker Tag *(10 minutes)* Try to create more Peacemakers than Fighters in a game of Tag.	
Live It! *(10 minutes)* Consider how they have to take steps to bring about peace.	• index card • pen

ILLUSTRATED BY RONNIE ROONEY

*Photocopy the Take-Home page at the end of this lesson for each child.

DEVOTIONS FOR LEADERS: PEACEMAKING

Peacemakers enter into conversations in helpful ways and bring resolution to difficult situations. How does that match the way you enter into conversations? Pay close attention to your conversations today. Do your words contribute to resolving difficulties or to making them worse? Pray that God would season your words with wisdom and grace so that you can bring peace to others today.

BIBLE BACKGROUND FOR LEADERS

Philemon 1:4-22: Onesimus Returns to Philemon

PAUL WRITES TO PHILEMON

Paul was in prison when he met Onesimus—a runaway slave—and led him to Jesus. Paul had previously led Onesimus' master, Philemon, to Jesus as well. And it was time for Onesimus to return to Philemon. So Paul wrote to Philemon to ask a favor. Paul asked Philemon to treat the return of his runaway slave as he would treat the return of a brother. In making his request, Paul expressed his gratitude for Philemon because he'd heard about Philemon's faith and love for God's people. Philemon's love had given Paul great comfort. "I could be bold and order you to do what you ought to do," wrote Paul. But instead, Paul made his request based on love and let Philemon decide what to do. Paul even offered to personally pay for anything Onesimus had taken from Philemon to smooth the way.

SMOOTHING THE WAY

As a fugitive slave, Onesimus could've been crucified—many slaves had been killed for doing far less than fleeing. Somehow, Onesimus had connected with Paul in Rome. Onesimus had become a Christian and proved to be useful to Paul. Paul's letter was designed to smooth the way for something that simply wasn't done in that day. Paul wanted master and slave to be reunited, not as property and property owner, but as brothers in Christ. Paul's letter was intended to bring peace into a very tense situation—a situation that Paul could've simply ignored. After all, he was in jail at the time. It's not as if he had nothing else to think about.

But Paul chose to get involved, to bring peace where there would otherwise be anger and violence.

THE LESSON

GOD SIGHTINGS

Use the standard text provided or substitute your own examples for this weekly lesson-starter activity.

Say: **God is with us everywhere! When your friend shares with you, you feel God's kindness. When you smile at a stranger and hold open a door, you're being God at work. A beautiful sunset is evidence of God's creativity and power. It's important that we recognize and thank God for all the things he does in our lives. We call these God Sightings.**

Ask: **What evidence have you seen of God at work this week? Think about God's creation, ways people have encouraged you, and even ways God helped you make a difference for someone else.**

Share your own God Sighting first. Then let kids share God Sightings—evidence of God in our world. Then celebrate how God is at work in your lives through a prayer of thanksgiving.

EXPLORE THE BIBLE!

Give each child a Bible, a pencil, and paper. Open your Bible to Philemon.

Talk about: **Onesimus came to help God's friend, Paul, while Paul was in prison. Unfortunately, there was a squabble. You see, Onesimus had run away from the man he worked for, so he was in trouble. Paul wrote a letter for Onesimus to take with him when he went home. Paul wanted to help bring peace to the relationship between Onesimus and Philemon, the man Onesimus worked for. Let's look at what Paul wrote.**

Read Philemon 1:4-22. Say: **Think of two friends of yours who've been in a fight. Write a letter (or draw a picture) that you could give them to encourage them to make**

YOU'LL NEED:

✓ Bibles
✓ pencils
✓ paper

LESSON 9 | WE BRING PEACE

peace. As you write, you can refer to these verses in Paul's letter for inspiration: **Philemon 1:8-10, 15-18.** Allow time for children to think and write. Help them read the verses as needed.

Lead this discussion: **What advice did you put in your letters? What did you learn from the verses you read in Paul's letter about bringing peace? What have you said or done to bring peace in the past?**

Talk about: **Paul brought peace to Philemon and Onesimus by pointing out to Philemon that Onesimus was helping Paul. Paul wrote that both Philemon and Onesimus were now Christians—brothers in the Lord. And Paul offered to help right any wrongs done to Philemon by Onesimus. We don't know how Philemon welcomed Onesimus. But if Paul's letter worked, it was a peaceful reunion. When we see squabbles,** *we bring peace*, **just as Paul did.**

STAND BY CLAY

YOU'LL NEED:
- ✓ Bible
- ✓ modeling clay

Say: **When Paul wrote to Philemon, he started out by expressing his thankfulness for Philemon and praising him for all the good he was doing. He was building Philemon up. Building each other up means encouraging each other and making people feel better.**

Talk about: **Tell about a time someone built you up.** Tell an example from your own life; then let kids share. **What can you do to build up someone else? How does building up people help bring peace?**

Say: **Building each other up makes good relationships from the beginning. The more we encourage each other, the less we'll squabble. We bring peace by encouraging others and building them up with kind words. There's also something good that happens to us!**

Read aloud Proverbs 12:20. Lead this discussion: **What does it mean to plan peace? When have you experienced joy because you helped other people get along?**

Distribute modeling clay, and let kids each make a friend named Clay. Then say: **Stand your new friend Clay on the table in front of you in any pose you choose. Close or cover your** left eye, and then hold up your right index finger in front of you. Line up your finger to the right of Clay so your finger and Clay look like they're right next to each other. Keep your head and your index finger absolutely still, but open your left eye as you close or cover your right eye.

Then lead this discussion: **What happened to your finger and Clay? Why? How is that like or unlike dealing with someone you're having a hard time getting along with? What's a way you could change the way you look at someone you're having a hard time with?**

Say: **When we look at people differently and take time to see their side of the story,** *we bring peace.*

DOG-EARED

Read aloud Proverbs 26:17: "Interfering in someone else's argument is as foolish as yanking a dog's ears."

Talk about: **What do you think this verse means? How do you know when to get involved in a conflict between two other people?**

Have kids get into pairs or trios, and distribute paper and pencils. Say: **In your pairs or trios, come up with a list of three to five conflicts that other people might have. Talk about if you might get involved. We'll use your ideas for our activity.** Allow time.

Ask groups to share the conflicts they listed. As they do, have kids tug on their ears if they think it would be foolish to get involved. Ask them to share any ideas they have for bringing peace to the situation.

Say: **Sometimes all we can do is pray for other people to see God in their situations. Other times, God gives us ways to help people understand each other. We can ask other Christians if we need help deciding a way** *we can bring peace.*

YOU'LL NEED:

✓ **Bible**
✓ **paper**
✓ **pencils**

LESSON 9 | WE BRING PEACE

PEACEMAKER TAG

Play a game of Tag to demonstrate how much we need peacemakers to help people stop fighting. Choose one person to be a Peacemaker and two to three people to be Fighters.

Have the Fighters hold hands. Say: **Imagine the Fighters want to drag others into their fight. If they tag another person, that person should hold their hands and join the chain. If the Peacemaker touches a link where two Fighters are holding hands, the Fighters should let go.**

Play several rounds, switching the roles of Fighters and Peacemaker.

Talk about: **Was it easier to spread the fight or to bring peace? In real life, what kinds of things make conflict spread quickly? What you can do to help bring peace more quickly?**

Say: **Sometimes it's easier to pick a side and join a fight, but we can listen to God and choose differently. When we do this,** *we bring peace.*

LIVE IT!

Have children stand in a line facing you, about 3 feet away from you. Talk about: **Bringing peace can be a step-by-step process, whether it's between other people you know or between you and someone else. You might not be able to fix a broken relationship with just a quick apology. But when we take some important steps,** *we bring peace.* **Let's experience that.**

If you've ever been mean to someone, turn around. Pause. **If you've ever said something that hurt someone's feelings, take a step away from me.** Pause. **If you've wished someone would leave you alone, take another step away.** Pause. **If you've ever not talked with someone because you were mad, take another step.** Pause.

Have kids turn back around. Hold up a card with the word "peace" written in small letters at the bottom, and ask kids to read it. They should be too far away to see that it says "peace."

YOU'LL NEED:

✓ **index card**
✓ **pen**

LEADER PREP

Write the word "peace" in small letters on an index card, near the bottom.

Say: **Let's see if you can get closer to this card so you can read the word. If you've ever smiled at someone, take a step forward.** Pause. **If you've listened to someone's point of view, take another step forward.** Pause. **If you've ever apologized to someone, take a step forward.** Pause. **If you've forgiven someone, take a step forward.** Pause. Then ask if kids can read the word.

Lead this discussion: **Tell about a time it took a while to fix an unpeaceful situation.**

Say: **When we're really angry, peace can seem far away. In our game, you got so far away from the word** *peace* **that you couldn't even read it. But each time we take a step toward peace, it becomes a little clearer. Step by step,** *we bring peace.*

PRAYER
Dear God, we know you want us to bring peace to one another. Help us be peacemakers. In Jesus' name, amen.

TAKE-HOME PAGE

Give each child a Take-Home page. Encourage kids to select one of the six challenges for the week ahead.

FOR LEADERS:
AVOIDING CONFLICT VS. BRINGING PEACE

Children can often tend toward avoiding conflict—because of their age and sometimes because of temperament. But avoiding conflict and bringing peace aren't always the same thing. When avoiding conflict prevents it from arising in the first place, it's a great thing. But when the conflict is already there, avoiding it keeps us from bringing true peace to the situation. Look for opportunities where a child is shrinking back from dealing with a difficult situation. Use that opportunity to shape that child's character by reminding him or her that to bring peace to a situation or relationship, we have to have the courage to face the conflict openly and honestly.

TAKE-HOME

PRACTICING PEACEMAKING

Keep growing in your faith and character. Choose one of the following challenges to do this week to grow in bringing peace.

CHALLENGE 1
Read Numbers 6:26; then quietly pray this blessing for someone you're having a hard time with right now. Think about how praying this blessing for that person affects how you feel toward him or her.

CHALLENGE 2
Find someone who needs to be encouraged, and think of something you can do to promote peace by building that person up. Then do it.

CHALLENGE 3
Draw a picture of the meeting between Philemon and Onesimus that shows what it might have looked like if Philemon welcomed Onesimus in the way Paul requested in his letter.

CHALLENGE 4
Read Acts 10:36, and think about what God did to bring you peace. Then pray, thanking God for his peace and asking him to show you what you can do to bring his peace to others.

CHALLENGE 5
Take a walk outside and find somewhere you think is peaceful. Draw or describe that place and what you think makes it peaceful. Then find two or three ways that drawing or description is like or unlike the peace we can bring to others.

CHALLENGE 6
Many proverbs use word pictures and comparisons to communicate a bigger concept or idea. In a notebook or journal, write your own proverb that uses a word picture or a comparison to communicate the importance of bringing peace to others. Look at Proverbs 12:20; Proverbs 14:30; and Proverbs 17:1 for examples. When you're done, share your proverb with a friend.

Permission to photocopy this resource from Grow Together Now, Volume 1 granted for local church use. Copyright © Group Publishing, Inc., 1515 Cascade Ave., Loveland, CO 80538.

JESUS WANTS US TO SERVE OTHERS

LESSON 10

LEADER PREP

Matthew 20:20-28

LESSON AT A GLANCE

James and John had their sights set high. They wanted to have places of honor with Jesus in his kingdom. But Jesus told them they were going about it the wrong way. In his kingdom, the places of honor are reserved for those who humble themselves and serve others here on earth. Use this lesson to help children serve others as Jesus wants.

SERVANT'S HEART IS... thinking of others before I think of myself.

WHAT KIDS DO	WHAT YOU'LL NEED
God Sightings *(5 minutes)* Talk about ways they've seen God at work.	
Explore the Bible! *(10 minutes)* Play a game about what they'd be willing to do for a prize.	• Bibles • kitchen timer • 1 chair for every child
Act It Out *(15 minutes)* Act out times they haven't put others first; then act out an alternative choice.	• Bible
Servant Sketch *(10 minutes)* Sketch qualities of a servant; then think about how they can be servants in their lives.	• copies of the handout *(found at the end of this lesson)* • colored pencils
Countdown *(10 minutes)* Practice taking turns, and discuss gifts they've been given for serving.	• Bibles
Live It! *(10 minutes)* Play a game about serving others.	• 1 chair for every child • 10 slips of paper for every chair • lively music

*Photocopy the Take-Home page at the end of this lesson for each child.

ILLUSTRATED BY RONNIE ROONEY

DEVOTIONS FOR LEADERS: A SERVANT'S HEART

We have people serve us every day. And seldom are they "important" people, pulling down high salaries in corner offices. They might include a cashier at a grocery story, a waiter at a restaurant, or a janitor at a school. But no matter who they are, they have one thing in common: In those moments that their lives intersect ours, they set their own needs aside to put our needs first. When that happens this week, ask God to speak to you about your own life of service. How are you doing at putting the needs of others before your own? How is God directing you to serve these days? Remember, when you serve others, you're serving him, too.

BIBLE BACKGROUND FOR LEADERS

Matthew 20:20-28: The Disciples Argue

A MOTHER'S REQUEST

The mother of James and John, two of Jesus' disciples, came to Jesus with a request. She wanted her sons to sit in places of honor next to Jesus in Jesus' kingdom. Jesus asked James and John, who had come with their mother, if they could drink from the same bitter cup of suffering he was about to drink from. They said they could. Jesus then told them that only God could determine who would be seated next to Jesus in heaven. The other 10 disciples were indignant when they heard what had been asked. So Jesus used the incident as an opportunity to teach all 12 disciples that, in his kingdom, whoever wanted to be a leader had to be a servant—just as Jesus was.

LEADERSHIP IS SERVANTHOOD

The disciples' indignation when James and John sought special privilege may've been jealousy…or a fear of losing out on a special privilege. Neither motivation pleased Jesus. The kingdom of God isn't a place where leadership is grasped through politics or displays of power. Rather, leadership in the kingdom of God is servanthood that's rewarded; it's humble submission to God. The kingdom of God operates on unusual values like honoring servants and making submission a leadership virtue. It doesn't really make sense until you realize that the kingdom of God has all the leadership it needs. It has God. What's in short supply are followers—those who willingly lay aside their own ambitions to be available for God's direction...whatever it might be.

THE LESSON

GOD SIGHTINGS

Use the standard text provided or substitute your own examples for this weekly lesson-starter activity.

Say: **God is with us everywhere! When your friend shares with you, you feel God's kindness. When you smile at a stranger and hold open a door, you're being God at work. A beautiful sunset is evidence of God's creativity and power. It's important that we recognize and thank God for all the things he does in our lives. We call these God Sightings.**

Ask: **What evidence have you seen of God at work this week? Think about God's creation, ways people have encouraged you, and even ways God helped you make a difference for someone else.**

Share your own God Sighting first. Then let kids share God Sightings—evidence of God in our world. Then celebrate how God is at work in your lives through a prayer of thanksgiving.

EXPLORE THE BIBLE!

Have kids help you place chairs in a circle. Hold a kitchen timer, and sit in one of the chairs. Say: **We're going to play a game. I don't really have a prize for you, but you need to play as if the winner gets a brand-new iPod. As soon as I start the timer and say "go," walk around the circle in Musical Chairs style. When the timer goes off, the person who sits in the chair on my right side wins!** Set the timer for different amounts each time as you play several rounds.

When the game is over, say: **Our Bible passage today is a lot like our game.** Read aloud Matthew 20:20-28.

Talk about: **Two of Jesus' friends—James and John—wanted to sit at Jesus' side in his kingdom. Jesus responded by**

YOU'LL NEED:

✓ Bible
✓ kitchen timer
✓ 1 chair for every child

LESSON 10 | JESUS WANTS US TO SERVE OTHERS

asking the two if they were ready to suffer the same way he would.

Explain that you're going to play the game again. Say: **This time we'll play the same way, but along with our pretend prize is a pretend price. If you win, you have to imagine you'd get the iPod, but not until you hang upside down from your toes while listening to the song that most annoys you—on repeat for an hour. If you don't think that'd be worth it, don't play.** Set the timer and see who still plays.

Lead this discussion: **How did you decide if the suffering would be worth it? How would you feel if you won the game and found out there was no prize but you still had to suffer?**

Talk about: **The disciples each wanted to be first. It's hard to serve others when we're just thinking about what we want. But to be first in Jesus' eyes, it takes a servant's heart.** *Jesus wants us to serve others.*

Leave the chairs in place for the Live It! activity.

ACT IT OUT

Say: **Most of us have a natural tendency to think of ourselves first. James and John's mother put her sons before anyone else.**

Have kids find partners. Say: **Think about a time you put yourself first. Without speaking, act out that incident. For example, if there was one cookie left and you snagged it before your brother could, act out grabbing and eating a cookie and then demonstrate the crying brother. See if your partner can guess your action.**

Allow a couple of minutes for kids to act. Alert them after one minute so both of them get a chance to act.

Then say: **Jesus said we need to change that thinking. He said whoever wants to be a leader needs to be a servant.**

Explain that kids will do the acting activity again. First, give these instructions: **Now think about how you can change your**

YOU'LL NEED:

✓ **Bible**

original action to show a servant's heart. For example, maybe you'll see that last cookie and smell that last cookie...and then offer it to your brother, who smiles and nods and pats his heart gratefully. **Act out a servant's heart.** Allow time, and again provide a signal at one minute.

Then lead this discussion: **Explain which comes more naturally to you: putting yourself or others first. When you notice you're acting selfish, what can help you change your thinking?**

Say: **Let's listen to a verse that explains how God wants us to treat others.**

Ask for a volunteer to read Philippians 2:3-4. Then talk about: **What do you think it means to think of others as better than yourself? How can thinking of others as better than yourself help you serve others?**

Ask for another volunteer to read aloud Luke 6:31. Then say: **It feels good to have others treat us as important. And Jesus wants us to treat others the same way we want to be treated. When we consider others better than ourselves, we put their needs above ours. And that helps us serve others.**

SERVANT SKETCH

Distribute handouts and colored pencils. Say: **In the top box on your handout, draw pictures representing what you think are the qualities and characteristics of a servant.** Allow time, and let kids share with a partner.

It's not easy to serve others. Sometimes it means totally changing the way we think. When we serve others, it shows that we don't think we're the most important. It doesn't show we think the other person is the most important either; it shows that Jesus is the One we want to serve.

Direct kids to the chart on the handout. Say: **Next to each location listed on the chart, write some ways you can be a servant in those locations.** Allow time and then ask for volunteers to share their responses.

YOU'LL NEED:

✓ **copies of the handout**
(found at the end of this lesson)

✓ **colored pencils**

LESSON 10 | JESUS WANTS US TO SERVE OTHERS

Say: *Jesus wants us to serve others*, and we encounter opportunities to serve others almost everywhere we go. Those opportunities can be big or small. They can be as simple as opening a door for someone or as big as cleaning up someone's yard. The size of the service isn't what matters. It's putting the needs of others first and making ourselves available that counts.

COUNTDOWN

Have everyone sit in a circle facing out. As a group, count backward from 10 to 1 as fast you can. Count out loud using the following rules:

- You can only speak to say numbers—no shouting.
- You can say just one number out loud before someone else says a number out loud.
- You can't go around the circle in order.
- If two people speak at the same time, start over.

Play at least two rounds. Then discuss what it was like to play this game. Talk about: **What happens when people always try to be first? How can taking turns help us serve others?**

Have kids form groups of three to five. Give each group a Bible, and have someone read 1 Peter 4:10. Say: **In your groups, discuss gifts you think God has given you. How can you use those gifts to serve others?**

Say: **Putting others first is a choice we make, and it is a way to serve. We each have been given gifts for serving.** *Jesus wants us to serve others.*

YOU'LL NEED:

✓ **Bibles**

LIVE IT!

Talk about: **Most of the time when we play games, we're trying to get or win something. For a change, let's play a game where the object is to give it all away.**

Have kids place chairs in a circle and stand behind them. Place 10 slips of paper on each child's chair. Say: **The object of this game is to get rid of all of your paper by putting it on someone else's chair. As others place paper on your chair, keep giving it away. But you can move only two papers at a time, and you can't stop someone from giving papers to you. Ready? Go!**

Play a song while children try to get rid of their papers. When the song ends, call time and determine the winner by counting the number of papers each child has. The child with the fewest slips of paper is the winner.

Lead this discussion: **What was it like to play this game? How's this game like or unlike serving others? Tell about someone you know who always seems to be serving others.** Give an example from your own life; then let kids share.

Talk about: **When we give of ourselves, we're serving them. In this game it seemed pretty hard for everyone to give all of the paper away, because people kept getting more paper even as they gave it away. Our lives are the same way. As we give of ourselves—as we serve—God uses the service of others to bring blessings and joy into our lives as well.** *Jesus wants us to serve others,* **and he honors those who do.**

PRAYER
Dear God, we know it pleases you when we put others first. Help us set aside our own desires so we can serve others. In Jesus' name, amen.

TAKE-HOME PAGE

Give each child a Take-Home page. Encourage kids to select one of the six challenges for the week ahead.

YOU'LL NEED:

✓ 1 chair for every child
✓ 10 slips of paper for each chair
✓ lively music

TAKE-HOME

PRACTICING PEACEMAKING

Keep growing in your faith and character. Choose one of the following challenges to do this week to grow in serving others just as Jesus wants.

CHALLENGE 1
Look for opportunities to let others go first today. You could open a door for someone, wait for someone else to get in line before you, or let others get their food first at your next meal.

CHALLENGE 2
Read Philippians 2:5-7. Then write or draw three things you can learn from Jesus about being a servant.

CHALLENGE 3
Think of ways you could give appreciation and encouragement to someone who serves others, such as your mom or dad, your pastor, or a first responder like a firefighter or ambulance driver. Then do it.

CHALLENGE 4
Read Galatians 5:13. Then write in a notebook or journal what you think that verse means for you.

CHALLENGE 5
Choose one of the ideas you listed for being a servant in different locations, and do it.

CHALLENGE 6
Use a phone directory or the internet to research service organizations or volunteer opportunities in your community. Then contact one that is of interest to you and find out how you can get involved.

A SERVANT LOOKS LIKE

I can be a servant by:

At home _____

At church _____

With friends _____

In sports _____

LESSON 10 | JESUS WANTS US TO SERVE OTHERS

WE CAN SERVE OTHERS AS JESUS DID

LESSON 11

LEADER PREP

John 13:1-17

LESSON AT A GLANCE

God's Son is perfect, powerful, and filled with love, but he humbled himself and became like a servant. He did a job that no one else thought about doing. He took water and a towel, and then he washed the dirty feet of his disciples. God's Son served in humble ways, and we can serve others just as he did. Use this lesson to help children develop a servant's heart.

SERVANT'S HEART IS... thinking of others before I think of myself.

WHAT KIDS DO	WHAT YOU'LL NEED
God Sightings *(5 minutes)* Talk about ways they've seen God at work.	
Explore the Bible! *(10 minutes)* Watch a video about Jesus washing feet.	• Bible • *Grow Together Now* DVD • DVD player
Dirty-Foot Snack *(15 minutes)* Make a servant snack and consider how to humble themselves.	• sugar-cookie wafers • chocolate cookie crumbs • bananas • raisins • paper plates • plastic knives • hand sanitizer
Return Serve *(10 minutes)* Serve snacks to those who serve in other classes.	• Dirty-Foot Snacks to share
Ball Control *(10 minutes)* Toss and catch balls as they learn about staying humble.	• Bible • small bouncy balls
Live It! *(10 minutes)* Create paper hands, and think of ways to use their real hands to help people.	• crayons • paper • scissors

*Photocopy the Take-Home page at the end of this lesson for each child.

ILLUSTRATED BY PAMELA JOHNSON

DEVOTIONS FOR LEADERS: A SERVANT'S HEART

It's amazing to think that Jesus, the Son of God, got on his knees in front of the disciples and washed their dirty, smelly feet. If Jesus could lower himself to the level of a common servant, then we as Christians can certainly humble ourselves and serve others. Be an example to kids and show what true service is all about—and encourage them to do the same for others.

BIBLE BACKGROUND FOR LEADERS

John 13:1-17: Jesus Washes the Disciples' Feet

A SIGNIFICANT ACTION

At the Last Supper recorded in John, it's especially significant that Jesus washed the disciples' feet, since none of the disciples was willing to stoop below the others to do this demeaning task. Since most people wore sandals in Bible times, servants washed guests feet before the beginning of any meal, or when a guest entered the house. However, since this was a private meal, apparently there was no servant there. Someone had provided the water, the basin, and the towel, and certainly the disciples must have thought about the fact that no one had washed their feet. But none of them took the initiative to do the washing before the meal. After the food had been set out, Jesus took action.

PETER'S OBJECTION

Peter's resistance to allowing Jesus to wash his feet revealed that Peter didn't understand what was really happening. He didn't yet understand that Jesus came to serve, not to be served. Peter's rejection of Jesus' act was based on an understanding of the Messiah that didn't allow for such a humble, servant-like action.

LEARNING HUMILITY

Jesus' final words in this passage are of particular importance. He explained to his disciples why he had humbled himself to wash their feet: He wanted them to do the same for others. Jesus emphasized the fact that no one is more important than anyone else—Christians are expected to humble themselves and serve each other.

THE LESSON

GOD SIGHTINGS

Use the standard text provided or substitute your own examples for this weekly lesson-starter activity.

Say: **God is with us everywhere! When your friend shares with you, you feel God's kindness. When you smile at a stranger and hold open a door, you're being God at work. A beautiful sunset is evidence of God's creativity and power. It's important that we recognize and thank God for all the things he does in our lives. We call these God Sightings.**

Ask: **What evidence have you seen of God at work this week? Think about God's creation, ways people have encouraged you, and even ways God helped you make a difference for someone else.**

Share your own God Sighting first. Then let kids share God Sightings—evidence of God in our world. Then celebrate how God is at work in your lives through a prayer of thanksgiving.

EXPLORE THE BIBLE!

Talk about: **Think about a time you were asked to do a really disgusting chore. Did you complain while you did it, or were you thankful you had a chance to help your parents out? Today we're going to learn about a dirty chore Jesus did. And we'll learn how** *we can serve others as Jesus did.* **Let's hear what Jesus did.**

Read aloud John 13:1-17. Then tell kids they'll see a fun video about what Jesus did. Show "Dirty Feet" (track 8) from the *Grow Together Now* DVD.

Lead this discussion: **Tell about a time your feet were really dirty and needed to be washed. Now think how you'd feel if the president or a celebrity washed those dirty feet. Say one word that expresses how you'd feel. What can you learn from the way Jesus served others in this situation?**

Talk about: **Jesus did something very strange in this passage. It wasn't usual for a leader or important teacher to do**

YOU'LL NEED:

✓ **Bible**
✓ ***Grow Together Now* DVD**
✓ **DVD player**

LESSON 11 | WE CAN SERVE OTHERS AS JESUS DID

YOU'LL NEED:

- ✓ sugar-cookie wafers
- ✓ chocolate cookie crumbs
- ✓ bananas
- ✓ raisins
- ✓ paper plates
- ✓ plastic knives
- ✓ hand sanitizer

ALLERGY ALERT

Consult with parents and be aware of any allergies the kids in your group might have.

LEADER PREP

Leave bananas in their peels and cut them in half. Each child will need half a banana, five raisins, and two sugar-cookie wafers. Have enough supplies so you can make extras to serve staff in your church office. Prepare chocolate cookie crumbs and keep them in a sealed container.

something that a servant normally did. But Jesus wanted to set an example of how we can all serve each other. Jesus is the ultimate servant because he laid down his life for us. And *we can serve others as Jesus did.*

DIRTY-FOOT SNACK

Talk about: **Jesus served his friends by cleaning their dirty feet. He put others first. Who's someone you know who seems to always put others first? What do you think about the idea of washing someone else's feet?**

Say: **We think of feet as dirty or maybe even smelly. Let's make a sweet snack to remember the feet Jesus so lovingly washed and how we can serve others.**

Give each child a paper plate with two sugar-cookie wafers, half of a banana, and five raisins. Set out plastic knives. Help kids each make a Dirty-Foot Snack with these steps:

1. Wash your hands.
2. Peel your banana half and slice it vertically so you have two sections.
3. Place a banana section "foot" on top of a sugar wafer "sandal." Cut banana to fit.
4. Arrange five raisins at the end of each banana section as "toes."
5. Sprinkle lightly with chocolate cookie crumb "dirt."

Ask kids who finish first to make extras for teachers in another nearby class. Set these aside.

Thank Jesus for being the perfect example of serving others. Then let everyone enjoy the snack.

Say: **The Dirty-Foot Snack reminds us to follow Jesus' example to be humble in all situations.** *We can serve others as Jesus did.*

RETURN SERVE

Talk about: **What are ways the teachers in our classes serve kids in church? What types of gifts did God give them for serving? How would it feel to serve them?**

Lead kids to nearby classrooms to share the snacks with teachers. Ask kids to explain the Dirty-Foot Snacks by telling about how Jesus washed his disciples' feet and calls on us to follow his lead and serve others. Then lead kids back to your room.

Say: **It feels good to serve others.** *We can serve others as Jesus did.*

YOU'LL NEED:

✓ **Dirty-Foot Snacks to share**

BALL CONTROL

Say: **Another way to describe serving others is the word** *humility.* **People who are humble don't mind serving. Let's see what the Bible tells us about being humble.**

Read aloud James 4:10. Ask kids what they think the verse means.

Distribute bouncy balls. Have kids sit on the floor. Give these instructions:

- **Stay seated and toss your ball as high as you can without hitting the ceiling, and catch it.**
- **Now toss your ball just a little lower and catch it.**
- **Continue tossing the ball lower and lower until you're barely getting it off your hands.**

Allow several minutes for kids to play. Then lead this discussion: **Which tosses were the hardest for you to catch? the easiest? How does lowering our pride help us be humble? What does it look like to be humble before God?**

Say: **The higher we toss a ball, the harder it is to catch it—because we have less control of it. It's important that we lower ourselves, making ourselves humble before the Lord. When we don't, we're kind of out of control and might hurt someone. Let's follow Jesus' example to be humble in all situations. Then** *we can serve others as Jesus did.*

YOU'LL NEED:

✓ **Bible**
✓ **small bouncy balls**

LESSON 11 | WE CAN SERVE OTHERS AS JESUS DID

YOU'LL NEED:

- ✓ paper
- ✓ crayons
- ✓ scissors

LIVE IT!

Have kids work together to trace their hands on paper with the crayons. Then say: **Think of some things you really need help with, such as cleaning your room, lifting something heavy, or reaching cookies on the top shelf. Write or draw one of those things on the palm of your traced hand.** Allow time.

When kids are finished, have them cut out their traced hands.

Once kids have their paper hands, have them get into groups of three. Say: **Talk about ways you can help each other with the things you need help with. When you've found a solution, write or draw it on the back side of your cutout hand. Ready? Let's give each other a hand!** Allow three minutes.

Lead this discussion: **Share how others helped you with your problem. How can you use your real hands to help other people? How can you lend a hand today to serve someone?**

Talk about: **There are many ways we can use our hands to help. We can pray** (fold your hands)**, we can lift** (lift your hands)**, or we can do something easy—like making people feel better** (give a thumbs-up or pat a child on the back)**. We serve people with our hands, and** *we can serve others as Jesus did.*

PRAYER
Thank you, God, for teaching us how to serve others and loving us just as we are. In Jesus' name, amen.

TAKE-HOME PAGE

Give each child a Take-Home page. Encourage kids to select one of the six challenges for the week ahead.

PRACTICING PEACEMAKING

Keep growing in your faith and character. Choose one of the following challenges to do this week to serve others as Jesus did.

CHALLENGE 1
Grab a box of paper clips, and make a paper-clip chain by adding a clip every time you serve someone. At the end of the week, show your chain to a parent or friend. Talk about all the ways God helped you serve others.

CHALLENGE 2
Put a friend or family member's shoes and socks on for him or her—even someone who already knows how to do it. Tell the person about when Jesus washed the disciples' feet. Explain that our feet don't get as dirty as the disciples' feet did because we have socks and closed shoes to protect them. Point out that Jesus did a really big service by washing those dirty feet.

CHALLENGE 3
Read about Jesus washing the disciples' feet with a family member. List all the ways Jesus served people. Then talk about who you can serve.

CHALLENGE 4
Apply James 4:10 by serving humbly—find ways to serve people without letting them know what you did. Maybe you'll help out at church, help around the house, or pray for someone who's sad. Pray and thank God for his help in serving others humbly.

CHALLENGE 5
Offer to be a 24-hour servant to someone in your family. Explain that for the whole day, you will be at his or her service and will help with whatever that person needs. Remember that Jesus wants us to be 24/7 servants. That means 24 hours a day, 7 days a week.

CHALLENGE 6
Offer to clean the soles of someone's dirty shoes or work boots. While you're working, think about how Jesus washed the disciples' feet to show them how to serve one another in helpful ways.

WE SERVE GOD WITH OUR FAMILY

LESSON 12

LEADER PREP

Joshua 24:14-18

SERVANT'S HEART IS... thinking of others before I think of myself.

LESSON AT A GLANCE

Joshua encouraged people to put away idols and to serve only God. Joshua said that he and his family would serve only God. He reminded the Israelites that God had brought their families out of slavery, protected them, worked miracles, and driven away their enemies. The people agreed to serve God, too! Use this lesson to help children learn to serve God with their families.

WHAT KIDS DO	WHAT YOU'LL NEED
God Sightings (5 minutes) Talk about ways they've seen God at work.	
Explore the Bible! (10 minutes) See God at the center of the family.	• Bibles • paper • markers or crayons
Service Wreaths (15 minutes) Make wreaths with ideas for how their families can serve God.	• poster board • paper • markers • scissors • pencils • glue
Rock-Solid Choice (10 minutes) Write about something God has done for their families.	• copies of the handout (found at the end of this lesson) • pens or pencils • large rocks (optional) • permanent markers (optional)
Gift Bags (10 minutes) Create gift bags for families to fill with toiletries for people in a homeless shelter.	• brown lunch bags • crayons or markers • small toiletries (optional)
Live It! (10 minutes) Watch a video about a serving family.	• *Grow Together Now* DVD • DVD player

ILLUSTRATED BY DANA REGAN

*Photocopy the Take-Home page at the end of this lesson for each child.

DEVOTIONS FOR LEADERS: A SERVANT'S HEART

Joshua's decision to serve God was for himself—and for his family. Based on what he'd seen, Joshua made a choice. He told the stories of deliverance, of God's provision, and of his mighty works. His family knew why Joshua served God and why they would, too. Why do you serve God? What "war stories" could you tell of God's blessing and deliverance? Think about your history with God, and make a mental or written list of the things he's done in your life. Then tell someone about them. Start with your family. You don't have to be near death the way Joshua was to tell your important stories of God's faithfulness. Choose today whom you will serve.

BIBLE BACKGROUND FOR LEADERS

Joshua 24:14-18: Joshua's Family Serves God

BELIEVE IT OR NOT

During Joshua's life, his world changed in ways he couldn't have imagined.

Born into slavery in Egypt, he witnessed the plagues, the first Passover, and the parting of the Red Sea. He tasted manna and watched Moses bring the Ten Commandments down from Mount Sinai. He spied out the Promised Land, wandered in the desert, crossed the Jordan, and led Israel to victory over the walled city of Jericho. If he hadn't lived it himself, he might not have believed it.

LIVING HISTORY

Israel's leaders had been with Joshua through the unbelievable. He said, "You have seen everything the Lord your God has done for you during my lifetime" (Joshua 23:3). Joshua was an old man—and he witnessed a new generation of Israelites living in peace and prosperity. Did they know God's mighty works had brought them here? He knew time was running out and called a meeting. He told the stories, beginning with Abraham's relocation to Canaan and God's promise of many descendants. He told about how those descendants ended up as slaves—and how God called Moses to a showdown with Pharaoh that ended with plagues and deliverance. As Joshua recounted great victories and battles of old, he wanted to remind people that everything they had was thanks to God (Joshua 24:2-13). The Israelites listened with rapt attention to Joshua's heroic tales. History became more than just an old story—it became reality—when told from an eyewitness perspective.

FAMOUS LAST WORDS

Joshua's story was a lot more than a history lesson. He made the case for people's continued service to God. In response to all that God had done, Joshua called his people to action: Honor God. Serve him with everything you have. Put away your idols. Serve only God. And then there was this unforgettable challenge: "But if you refuse to serve the Lord, then choose today whom you will serve…But as for me and my family, we will serve the Lord."

THE LESSON

GOD SIGHTINGS

Use the standard text provided or substitute your own examples for this weekly lesson-starter activity.

Say: God is with us everywhere! When your friend shares with you, you feel God's kindness. When you smile at a stranger and hold open a door, you're being God at work. A beautiful sunset is evidence of God's creativity and power. It's important that we recognize and thank God for all the things he does in our lives. We call these God Sightings.

Ask: What evidence have you seen of God at work this week? Think about God's creation, ways people have encouraged you, and even ways God helped you make a difference for someone else.

Share your own God Sighting first. Then let kids share God Sightings—evidence of God in our world. Then celebrate how God is at work in your lives through a prayer of thanksgiving.

LESSON 12 | WE SERVE GOD WITH OUR FAMILY

YOU'LL NEED:

- ✓ Bibles
- ✓ paper
- ✓ markers or crayons

EXPLORE THE BIBLE!

Talk about: **We can each help decide how our families will serve God. In the Bible, Joshua and his people had a choice: Would they serve God or the fake gods other people worshipped? We can make the same choice Joshua did and say** *we serve God with our family.*

Have a child read aloud Joshua 24:14. Say: **Then Joshua spoke to all his people and gave them an important choice.** Have another child read aloud Joshua 24:15.

Say: **You've just heard the choice Joshua gave his people. Our families have the same choice today.** Distribute paper and crayons or markers. **Create a picture of yourself and your family, leaving the middle of the page blank.** Allow about four minutes.

Say: **Listen to how the people responded to Joshua.** Have a child read aloud Joshua 24:16-17. Say: **The people remembered everything God did for them. And they made a decision.** Read aloud Joshua 24:18.

Have kids roll their papers into tubes and stare at a light for 30 seconds through the tubes. Say: **This represents the light God brings into our lives.** Have kids unroll their papers and look at their family pictures. They'll see a residual image of the light in the center.

Say: **God deserves to be at the center of our lives just like the image you see now in the center of your family.** Have kids write or draw "God" in the center of their papers.

Lead this discussion: **Why do you think God gives us the choice of whether or not to serve him? Why do you think it's important that we make the choice to serve only God? What are ways your family serves God now?**

Talk about: **Joshua told everyone who'd listen about the amazing things God had done for his family—and then he told people that there's no other god he and his family would serve. Like Joshua and his people, your family can decide together to serve God.**

SERVICE WREATHS

Talk about: Joshua was a man who served God faithfully along with his family. What are things that could distract your family from serving God? How can you help your family stay focused on serving God?

Say: **When we keep our focus on God, it's easier for families to serve God together. When we're distracted, it makes it hard to do what Joshua and his family did—work together to serve God. We can learn to resist distractions so *we can serve God with our families.***

Let's make a craft that you can take home to help your family focus on serving God. Gather kids around supplies. Guide them in making service wreaths by following these steps:

1. Trace the outline of your left and right hands onto sheets of paper.

2. Cut out several sets of hand shapes.

3. On each hand, write an act of service your family can do together for your church, a missionary, or another family.

4. Place the handprints, fingers out, in a circle and glue them to the poster board.

5. Share the wreath ideas with your family, and hang it where everyone can see it.

Say: **Joshua wanted people to choose to serve only God. Joshua made the choice that he and his family would serve God. Like Joshua, you can serve God with your family.**

YOU'LL NEED:

✓ **poster board**
✓ **paper**
✓ **markers**
✓ **scissors**
✓ **glue**
✓ **pencils**

LESSON 12 | WE SERVE GOD WITH OUR FAMILY

YOU'LL NEED:

✓ **copies of the handout** (found at the end of this lesson)

✓ **pens or pencils**

LEADER PREP

For extra impact, bring in large rocks and permanent markers for kids to decorate.

YOU'LL NEED:

✓ **brown paper lunch bags**

✓ **crayons or markers**

✓ **small toiletries** (optional)

ROCK-SOLID CHOICE

Distribute handouts and pens or pencils. Ask older kids to help younger kids by pairing up.

Say: **Joshua made an important choice in today's Bible lesson. At the top of your handout, write something you remember about Joshua's choice.** Allow time.

Continue: **Now think about something God has done for your family in the past year, such as providing a fun vacation or helping them through a tough time. Draw or describe on the rock** (on the handout, or on an actual rock if available) **what God did for your family.** Allow time, and encourage kids to share their drawings with a partner or the group.

Lead this discussion: **Why is serving God as a family a good or "rock solid" choice? Why do you think it's sometimes hard for families to serve God? What would it look like for your family to say, "But as for me and my family, we will serve the Lord"?**

Let kids work independently on the remaining questions on their handouts:

- How would it change your family to serve God together?
- How can you help your family make the choice to serve God this week?

Say: **Joshua remembered what God had done for him and the people of Israel. He responded by choosing to serve God. You can make the same choice and serve God with your family. Show your family your rock and talk with your family about how God has blessed you and how you can serve God together.**

GIFT BAGS

Set out paper lunch bags and crayons or markers, and gather kids around the supplies.

Talk about: **Some people in our town have nowhere to live, so they may be in a homeless shelter. One way to serve them with your family is to share supplies they might need.**

What kinds of items would be helpful for a person who has no home? Think of things *you* use every day. How do you think it would make people feel to receive a bag of supplies from a family in the area?

Have kids decorate the bags with cheerful designs. If the contents of the bag are specifically intended for a man or woman, have kids indicate that at the top of the bag. Provide any small toiletries you may have collected in advance to get kids started. Encourage kids to fill the bags with small items from a discount store and deliver as a family to a local homeless shelter.

Pray together for the people who'll receive the bags, asking God to bless each person.

LIVE IT!

Talk about: **In the Bible, Joshua said that he and his family would serve God. Serving God with your family doesn't always have to mean something big, like building houses in Africa or raising a million dollars for charity. It can mean helping people right in your own town. Watch as one family serves God together.**

Show "The Family That Serves" (track 9) from the *Grow Together Now* DVD.

Lead this discussion: **What did you learn from this family about serving? How does your family serve together?**

Talk about: **A great way to serve God with your family is to help other people.** *We serve God with our family,* **and an easy way to do that is to look for ways to help people right in our own town or neighborhood!**

PRAYER
Thank you, God, for our families and for the opportunities we have to serve God together. In Jesus' name, amen.

TAKE-HOME PAGE

Give each child a Take-Home page. Encourage kids to select one of the six challenges for the week ahead.

LEADER PREP

Help get the family gift bags started, if possible, with a few toiletries purchased at discount stores. Gather information about local homeless shelters, and share this with families along with ideas for completing and distributing the bags.

YOU'LL NEED:

✓ *Grow Together Now* DVD
✓ DVD player

TAKE-HOME

PRACTICING PEACEMAKING

Keep growing in your faith and character. Choose one of the following challenges to do this week to serve God with your family.

CHALLENGE 1
Choose something that can distract you from serving God with your family, and give it up for the week.

CHALLENGE 2
Think of one thing you've never done before to serve God, and do it. Ask a family member to do it with you.

CHALLENGE 3
Volunteer to help a parent with a task. As you're working together, ask your parent to tell you about a time God sent another family to serve your family.

CHALLENGE 4
Read aloud Joshua 24:14-18 as if you were Joshua speaking to the people of Israel. Then create a list of all the ways God has blessed your family. If you're feeling brave, gather everyone together in the living room and remind them of all the blessings—and then challenge them to serve God with you.

CHALLENGE 5
Take a walk around the outside of your house. As you do, pray for your family members, asking God to help you serve him together. Then go into each room and think of a way you can serve God in that room. For instance, if the room has a computer, you could serve God by writing letters to people who are discouraged.

CHALLENGE 6
Use carrot sticks, lettuce, cheese, and other veggies to create individual "House Salads" to serve each family member at dinner. Pray before the meal, and ask God to help your family "house" serve him.

Permission to photocopy this resource from Grow Together Now, Volume 1 granted for local church use. Copyright © Group Publishing, Inc., 1515 Cascade Ave., Loveland, CO 80538.

Joshua's choice:
_____
_____
_____

God has helped my family

How would it change your family to serve God together?
_____
_____
_____

How can you help your family make the choice to serve God this week?
_____
_____
_____

WE SERVE EVERYONE

LESSON 13

LEADER PREP

LESSON AT A GLANCE

Jesus told a parable about a Samaritan who showed mercy to a Jewish man who'd been attacked and beaten and was lying on the side of the road. The Samaritan stopped, bandaged the man's wounds, and paid for him to stay in an inn. God wants us to serve people whether they're next door, across the street, or in another country. Use this lesson to help children learn to serve everyone.

Luke 10:30-37

SERVANT'S HEART IS... thinking of others before I think of myself.

WHAT KIDS DO	WHAT YOU'LL NEED
God Sightings *(5 minutes)* Talk about ways they've seen God at work.	
Explore the Bible! *(10 minutes)* Watch a video about the good Samaritan.	• Bibles • *Grow Together Now* DVD • DVD player
Hard to Handle *(10 minutes)* Struggle with some papers and not others.	• strips of paper • pens or pencils • tape
Sam Meets Pigs *(15 minutes)* Rewrite a classic fairy tale to include the good Samaritan.	• "The Three Little Pigs" story, online or in a book • copies of the handout *(found at the end of this lesson)* • pencils
Spider Web Races *(10 minutes)* Go through a maze, and discuss helping others when it's inconvenient.	• various tables and chairs • yarn • stopwatch
Live It! *(10 minutes)* Explore whether people around the globe are neighbors, as Jesus defines them.	• map or globe

ILLUSTRATED BY PAIGE BILLIN-FRYE

*Photocopy the Take-Home page at the end of this lesson for each child.

119

DEVOTIONS FOR LEADERS: A SERVANT'S HEART

Jesus was intentional about casting the Samaritan as the hero. He wanted to show the Jewish people that "neighbor" surpasses borders. A neighbor can be anyone, without regard to nation, religion, or proximity. How does that definition of neighbor change the way you serve others? Do you serve those you know more easily than those you don't? Challenge yourself this week to look beyond borders and past prejudices to serve people in need.

BIBLE BACKGROUND FOR LEADERS

Luke 10:30-37: The Good Samaritan

LOADED QUESTIONS

Wherever Jesus went, questions followed. Some were sincere, as in "Can you heal my child?" or "How will we feed all these people?" Others were loaded, meant to weaken Jesus' authority or find grounds for his crucifixion. Two men, a rich man and an "expert" in religious law, asked the same question two separate times: "Teacher, what must I do to receive eternal life?" (Matthew 19:16; Luke 10:25). One asked honestly; the other asked as a test.

LOADED ANSWERS

Jesus answered both men by the law and commandments, including in his answer, "Love your neighbor as yourself." The religious expert, however, wouldn't leave it at that. "The man wanted to justify his actions, so he asked Jesus, 'And who is my neighbor?' " (Luke 10:29). To the Jews, the word *neighbor* meant members of the Hebrew nation only—no outsiders. So when the expert asked, "And who is my neighbor?" he wasn't asking out of ignorance. He was hoping Jesus would confirm what the Jews believed.

ILLUSTRATED BY DANA REGAN

A TELLING STORY

Instead, Jesus answered with a story about a Jewish man. While traveling a dangerous and desolate road, the man was attacked. Bandits stripped him of his clothes, took his money, and beat him until he was almost dead. They left the man, bruised and bleeding, to die on the side of the road. His hope of rescue was slim at best, but "by chance a priest came along." *Ah, the hero!* the expert likely thought. Imagine his surprise when Jesus said the priest avoided the man and passed him by. A Temple assistant also came upon the scene, but he only gawked for a moment and then passed by as well.

AN UNLIKELY HERO

"Then a despised Samaritan came along." Anyone listening to Jesus would know the history and hatred that clouded the Jewish-Samaritan relationship. Surely the Samaritan too would pass by. But Jesus revealed a plot twist: "When he saw the man, he felt deep pity." The Samaritan showed compassion, not only in how he felt about the man but also in his actions. He soothed the man's pain, bandaged his wounds, removed him from the roadside, and took him on his donkey to an inn. The Samaritan even paid extra to ensure care for the man would continue after he left. "Which of these three would you say was a neighbor?" Jesus asked. The answer was clear, but the expert in religious law couldn't bring himself to identify the Samaritan by name as the hero of the story. He simply replied, possibly through gritted teeth, "The one who showed him mercy."

THE LESSON

GOD SIGHTINGS

Use the standard text provided or substitute your own examples for this weekly lesson-starter activity.

Say: **God is with us everywhere! When your friend shares with you, you feel God's kindness. When you smile at a stranger and hold open a door, you're being God at work. A beautiful sunset is evidence of God's creativity and power. It's important that we recognize and thank God for all the things he does in our lives. We call these God Sightings.**

Ask: **What evidence have you seen of God at work this week? Think about God's creation, ways people have encouraged you, and even ways God helped you make a difference for someone else.**

Share your own God Sighting first. Then let kids share God Sightings—evidence of God in our world. Then celebrate how God is at work in your lives through a prayer of thanksgiving.

LESSON 13 | WE SERVE EVERYONE

YOU'LL NEED:

- ✓ Bible
- ✓ *Grow Together Now* DVD
- ✓ DVD player

EXPLORE THE BIBLE!

Say: **Jesus often told stories to teach people things. When teaching people about being nice to neighbors, Jesus told this story about a Jewish man and a man from Samaria.**

Read aloud Luke 10:30-37.

Say: **Now let's watch and see what happens to the Jewish man on the road to Jericho.**

Show "The Good Samaritan" (track 10) on the *Grow Together Now* DVD.

Lead this discussion: **What do you think about how the three men treated the hurt man? Tell about a time someone helped you when you needed it.** Give an example from your own life; then let kids share. **Tell which man you're most like when someone different from you needs help.**

Talk about: **Samaritans and Jews were sort of enemies, but even that didn't stop the Samaritan man from helping. *We serve everyone* because God wants us to—even if they're different from us. If someone needs our help, we help them!**

HARD TO HANDLE

Say: **Jesus told about a hurt man who was lying beside the road needing help. Many people who could've helped just walked on by, but the good Samaritan helped.**

Give kids each 6 to 10 strips of paper. Say: **Try to pick up the strips of paper using just a pen or pencil. As you're doing this, think about a neighbor who's difficult to serve.** Explain that kids are not to stab the papers. Allow time.

Now have kids tape half of the strips in loops. Let them try to pick up the papers again.

Lead this discussion: **How did the differences in the papers make them easier or harder to pick up? What can make people in your life hard to handle or difficult to serve? Rather than ignoring people you don't like or giving up on**

YOU'LL NEED:

- ✓ strips of paper
- ✓ pens or pencils
- ✓ tape

people who are difficult, how can you respond to them the way the good Samaritan did?

Say: **Just like the two types of paper strips were different, people are all different, too. Some can be difficult.** *We serve everyone* **because God wants us to, not because it's easy.**

SAM MEETS PIGS

Say: **The Samaritan was a good neighbor. He showed mercy by serving someone in need and helping him when others ignored him.**

Tell a partner about a time you helped someone. Allow time; then continue. **Next, talk with your partner about this: How would you describe a neighbor? What is a neighbor?**

Gather kids back together and read the simple fairy tale "The Three Little Pigs."

Then distribute handouts and ask kids to write ways the story might change if the good Samaritan had entered the scene. Allow several minutes for writing.

Lead this discussion: **In what specific ways might the Samaritan serve the characters in the story? Who are people you know who may need the same kind of help? How can you be a kind neighbor like the Samaritan?**

Say: **Our neighbors may be nearby or far away. The man who the Samaritan helped wasn't even from the same town. The Samaritan helped him because he knew that** *we serve everyone* **because God wants us to.**

YOU'LL NEED:

✓ **"The Three Little Pigs" story, online or in a book**

✓ **copies of the handout** *(found at the end of this lesson)*

✓ **pencils**

LESSON 13 | WE SERVE EVERYONE

YOU'LL NEED:

- ✓ **various tables and chairs**
- ✓ **yarn**
- ✓ **stopwatch**

YOU'LL NEED:

- ✓ **map or globe**

SPIDER WEB RACES

Choose an area of the room where there are lots of tables and chairs, and remove anything breakable.

Have kids drape and tangle yarn over, up, under, behind, and through the area until you have a web that's a challenge to get through.

Time each person to see how long it takes to make it through the web without touching any of the yarn.

Lead this discussion: **How did the spider web keep you from getting from one side of the room to the next? In life, what things keep you from stopping to help others?**

Say: **Like the good Samaritan,** *we serve everyone,* **even if it means going out of our way to do so.**

LIVE IT!

Talk about: **What makes someone a neighbor?** Allow a few minutes for kids to discuss.

Show kids a map or globe, and point to where you are now. Say: **We live here. Is the person who lives here** (point to a place close to where you live) **our neighbor?** Let the kids respond. **Is the person who lives over here** (point to another country on the globe) **our neighbor?** Let the kids respond. **How can someone who lives far away still be our neighbor?** Allow time for kids to discuss.

Pick a child to twirl around three times and then place his or her hand on the map or globe. Say: **People in other countries are just like people right here; they still need help sometimes. Let's come up with three ways we can serve or help people in that country—right from where we are.** Allow a few minutes for kids to brainstorm.

Lead this discussion: **What do you think might be different about people in the country you chose from people in our country? What do you think might be the same? When you see someone who needs help, how do you decide whether** to help? What's one thing you'll do to serve or help someone far away this week?

Talk about: **People near and far need help sometimes. It doesn't matter who they are or where they live. We have neighbors all over the globe, and we can find creative ways to bless God by serving and helping them.** *We serve everyone.*

PRAYER
Thank you, God, for making us all unique and special, for loving us just the way we are, and for giving us opportunities to serve each other. In Jesus' name, amen.

TAKE-HOME PAGE

Give each child a Take-Home page. Encourage kids to select one of the six challenges for the week ahead.

LESSON 13 | WE SERVE EVERYONE

TAKE-HOME

PRACTICING PEACEMAKING

Keep growing in your faith and character. Choose one of the following challenges to do this week to serve your neighbor.

CHALLENGE 1
Read about the good Samaritan in Luke 10:30-37. Make a supply of bandages that say, "God loves you!" on each wrapper. Carry one with you all the time. When someone needs a bandage or encouragement, serve him or her. Hand that person a bandage and say, "God loves you."

CHALLENGE 2
Follow the good Samaritan's example and go out of your way to serve three different people today. Then talk to your parents about who you helped and how you helped them.

CHALLENGE 3
Talk to the teachers at your church, and offer to be a good Samaritan by sending postcards or notes to kids who are sick, new, or haven't been in church lately.

CHALLENGE 4
Look for ways to serve your neighbors by doing things like sweeping their walkways, helping them carry groceries, or hauling their trash cans from the curb.

CHALLENGE 5
Choose someone you wouldn't normally help—a little brother, an older sister, a grumpy neighbor—and do something special to serve that person today.

CHALLENGE 6
Spin the globe and choose a country to be your "neighbor." Throughout the day, pray for the people and missionaries in that country.

SAM MEETS PIGS

_____
_____
_____
_____
_____
_____
_____
_____
_____
_____

LESSON 13 | WE SERVE EVERYONE